THE
WORLD
IN MY
MIRROR

# MARGARET JEAN JONES

# THE WORLD IN MY MIRROR

Abingdon

Nashville

THE WORLD IN MY MIRROR

*Copyright © 1979 by Abingdon*

**Library of Congress Cataloging in Publication Data**

JONES, MARGARET JEAN.
  The world in my mirror.
    1.  Jones, Margaret Jean.   2.   Christian biography—United States.   3.   Paraplegia—Biography. I. Title.
BR1725.J645A38      248'.2[B]               79-17730

*ISBN 0-687-46270-3*

Scripture quotations unless otherwise noted are from the King James Version of the Bible. Those noted RSV are from the Revised Standard Version of the Bible, copyright 1946, 1952, © 1971, 1973 by the Division of Christian Education of the National Council of the Churches of Christ in the U.S.A.; those noted NEB are from the New English Bible. © the Delegates of the Oxford University Press and the Syndics of the Cambridge University Press 1961, 1970; those noted TEV are from the Bible in Today's English Version, copyright © American Bible Society 1966, 1971, 1976; those noted Phillips are from the New Testament in Modern English, copyright © J. B. Phillips, 1958, 1959, 1960, 1972; those noted TJB are from the Jerusalem Bible, copyright © 1966 by Darton, Longman & Todd, Ltd. and Doubleday & Company, Inc; those noted TLB are from *The Living Bible,* copyright © 1971 Tyndale House Publishers, Wheaton, Illinois; those noted TAB are from the Amplified Old and New Testament, © The Lockman Foundation, 1958. Zondervan Publishing House; those noted NAS are from the New American Standard, © The Lockman Foundation, 1960, 1962, 1963, 1968, 1971, 1972. World Publishing, Times Mirror, N.Y.

The poetry by Jane Merchant is from her books, *Think About These Things* and *The Mercies of God,* and is used by permission of Abingdon.

MANUFACTURED BY THE PARTHENON PRESS AT
NASHVILLE, TENNESSEE, UNITED STATES OF AMERICA

## TO MY BELOVED FAMILY AND FRIENDS

Whose love and encouragement have inspired me
to rekindle my faith and renew my trust in God

# CONTENTS

Preface.................................................. 9

Another Rent in the Tapestry of Life................11

The Monster............................................. 18

Life as a Horizontal.................................... 25

Bitter or Better?....................................... 32

High Hopes...............................................41

Exhibit "A" in a Bikini................................ 46

Birthday Boulevard...................................... 52

Through the Looking Glass...............................58

My Angel Mother......................................... 66

Waxing Eloquent......................................... 74

Resources and Resourcefulness...........................79

Rehabilitation from Within.............................. 86

Victim or Victor?....................................... 90

Monument or Stumbling Block?............................ 97

When God Opens Doors....................................102

A New Dimension............................................ 112

Like the Breath of a Rose............................. 116

The Book of Life............................................ 123

Rigid But Not Unyielding.............................. 127

A Stone of Help.............................................. 132

Out of Weakness Strength............................. 138

Choose Life..................................................... 151

# PREFACE

My dear friend and former pastor, the Rev. James Masters, is not one to take no for an answer, not even sometimes.

"When," he asked one day as he sat leafing through my second book on the history of my native Cullman County, Alabama, "are you going to write an inspirational book?"

"Well," I replied hesitantly, "many people have asked me that, but there are already so many outstanding books in that category."

"Yes," he agreed, "but you won't be trying to compete. You will simply be telling your own personal experience of a walk of faith which could touch and inspire the lives of many people."

"Nobody would be interested in my ups and downs and my trials and problems," I started to protest.

But then the truth of what he was trying to get across began to dawn on me. I would not be writing the book to tell about my pains; I would be writing the book to tell what God had shown me and what he was continuing to do for me. I thought about this and pondered the idea: If God can be glorified and I can be a tool to accomplish that, then it should be done.

The apostle Paul didn't write in an air-conditioned office surrounded by conveniences. What he wrote was often written under the most difficult of circumstances—before, during, and after stoning, before, during, and after shipwrecks—yet he wrote. And so with the encouragement of his assurance to the Corinthian Christians that ". . . if there be first a willing mind, it is accepted according to that a man hath, and not according to that he hath not," I began to write this book in an attempt to express something of the triumphs that are to be found through a total reliance on God's amazing grace and power.

It is truly my prayer that somewhere within these pages you, dear reader, will experience anew, or perhaps for the first time, the strength of God's everlasting arms which endures in all things.

*Margaret Jean Jones*

*Beloved, think it not strange*
*concerning the fiery trial which*
*is to try you. (I Pet. 4:12)*

# ANOTHER RENT
# IN THE TAPESTRY OF LIFE

For the second time in twenty-two years, crushing circumstances beyond my control were disrupting my life right before my eyes. There wasn't a thing I could do except stare straight ahead. Hot tears stung my eyes, and I shut them tightly. Youthful dreams had been shattered long years ago; adjustments had been made, and I'd come to grips with the harsh realities of my situation. And not mine only, my condition affected the lives of my parents in a way that was to alter their life-style forever.

In January 1954, at the age of seventeen and just out of high school, the invasion of a vicious monster in the form of a rare and mysterious disease had left me totally paralyzed and permanently confined to bed. Now, in December 1975, I was facing the need to move into a nursing home because my mother, who had faithfully nursed me night and day single-handedly until only a year earlier, was in rapidly failing health. She was no longer able to take over even during the evening when the part-time hired attendants had left, and full-time nursing care was not available.

Possessed by a naturally ingrained and unquench-
ably ambitious nature, throughout my life I had
pursued whatever resources were left to me along
with the latent talents God had entrusted to my care.
Looking over my life, what emerged was a rather
complex mosaic. Much painful trial and error, along
with more than a little ignorance, had gone into
developing and nurturing that Christian faith which
enabled me to find fulfillment in life. My days had
been enriched by two factors: First, my pursuit of a
career as a free-lance magazine writer; and second,
my maintenance of a genuine interest in everything
that went on around me even though I could not be an
active part of it. Added to this was my keen interest
in people. Now it appeared that the hard-won
victories might very well be coming to an end.

I had been able to pursue a writing career only
because my devoted mother took time from her many
household responsibilities and the nursing duties
required for just my physical care to set up my
typewriter and insert a fresh sheet of paper each time
I finished a page. At other times she would have to
research materials for me. She was my arms, my
legs—the body in motion that I could not be. I knew
there would be nobody at a nursing home who would
so devotedly do for me what my mother had always
done. I could, of course, continue to write first drafts
in longhand provided someone gave me the paper and
the pencils. Still, I was totally dependent upon
others.

A steady stream of fascinating people from all
walks of life frequently came to our house through
the years. What a privilege it was to meet these
individuals and to form warm friendships. Much of

this was a result of my newspaper column and two books on local history which I'd had the joy and satisfaction of writing. We didn't keep visiting hours at our house. We could entertain guests at their convenience and ours. Institutional care, I sensed, would not allow for that kind of freedom. I could understand the need for a more structured routine which such a place would require. At home I was one person for my mother to care for; at the nursing home there would be many people needing attention from a limited staff.

It had been these many new friends, along with faithful long-time friends and loving relatives, who helped so much to broaden my horizons beyond the bedroom walls and keep alive my interest in the outside world. The leisurely and stimulating conversations I often enjoyed with these visitors were certain to be, of necessity, more limited, subdued, and abbreviated in a nursing home atmosphere.

But this new rent in my life's tapestry would have to be dealt with later. My immediate priority was how to cope with the emotional trauma of leaving behind, possibly forever, the beloved farm I shared with my parents and which I had called home for thirty-five years. Looking out my bedroom window countless times daily for the twenty-two years I'd been bedfast, I'd come to know and love every inch of my father's pastures and pond as well as the lovely old homeplace on the hill above our house. It was all clearly visible from my bed.

The giant oak tree outside the window afforded quiet companionship as did the birds that flitted through its branches. The squirrels that scampered playfully under and in the trees were my friends.

Although the serene beauty and the inspiration I received from observing the changing scenery of God's handiwork would be indelibly stamped upon my memory forever, I would miss the beloved and familiar surroundings terribly.

I entered the Hanceville Nursing Home, located about twenty miles from our farm, one week before Christmas in 1975. It was an ironic climax to an incredible year that had seen my hospitalization for major surgery—canceled at the last minute by doctors. There had also been the publication of my second book on local history and several awards from civic clubs for my efforts in historical preservation.

But that wasn't all. Less than two weeks before, I had been the guest of honor at the formal opening of the Margaret Jean Jones Adult Activities Center for the handicapped in Cullman. The naming of it in my honor had come as a stunning surprise. The officers and board of directors, of which I was a charter member and past president, had worked hard for five long years to make this much-needed facility for the severely handicapped a reality. The privilege of cutting the ribbons, which were held in place by the mayor and county commission chairman, was certainly one of the biggest highlights of my life.

After all that heady excitement, the sudden change of environment was going to be even more dramatic than I could have possibly imagined. The fact that I had known vaguely for some time that there was a distinct possibility that I would have to go live in a nursing home someday, if I lived that long, hadn't really prepared me for the actual transition.

My family, all of whom had been devastated by the

developments that necessitated my going to the nursing home, were even more distraught by the timing. Both sides of our family are closely knit and Christmas has always been a time for big family get-togethers complete with much merrymaking, groaning tables of food, and groaning people who invariably eat too much.

I knew, for my family's sake as well as my own, that I had to somehow find the strength not to fall into a state of depression. Initially it was I who had called the owner of the nursing home in August to request a room as soon as one became available. The owner was a friend of my father's, and this helped to lift our sagging spirits some. My aunt, who had been helping mother with my care, developed a heart condition and could no longer help us. We felt very fortunate when we found a lady to come in for a couple hours each morning. For a short time my mother's chronic lung condition seemed to be improving. Our hopes soared—maybe I wouldn't have to go to the nursing home after all.

Then, early in November, mother's problems were suddenly compounded when rheumatoid arthritis struck her body viciously leaving her barely able to walk. She was left with practically no strength whatsoever in her hands and arms. My heart was broken—Mother, who had so lovingly and patiently ministered to my every need for so long now needed someone to care for her. As her daughter my heart ached to do for her as she had always done for me. My father, as usual, was the Rock of Gibraltar. But it was just too much for him to care for two women.

The move to a nursing home was now urgent, but Daddy was adamant that I should not go before the

open house ceremonies for the Activities Center. He
was determined that I attend. That in itself would be
a major undertaking. I had not been out of the house
for more than two years. We were not certain
whether the nursing home staff could or would be
able to get me dressed and give the routine care that
was required, all in time for me to attend the
festivities. When my father explained the situation,
Mr. Moody promised to have a room available the
week following the open house.

I urged Daddy not to tell our family and friends
about my going to the nursing home until after the
celebration ceremonies. The board members had
gone all out to make this a gala occasion and, at the
same time, focus public attention on the hoped-for
goals we had set for the center and our dreams of a
more fulfilling life for the severely handicapped
people who would use the center. Friends on the
board had even made special arrangements with the
Cullman County Rescue Squad ambulance crew to
transport me to the event.

Daddy's heart was just as broken as Mother's and
mine—perhaps even more so. He finally broke down
and confided in family members his great concern.
They, in turn, quietly spread the word around.
Everyone was striving valiantly to conceal their
knowledge, but I sensed that they knew. Finally, in
an effort to inject some humor into the situation, my
younger cousin Diann, who had spent many happy
hours playing word games with me during her teen
years, asked wryly, "Can we turn off this happiness
bit after the open house is over?" To my relatives' and
friends' credit, their smiles were as radiant as those
of the more than four hundred other guests who

came to make the day a grand success for all in-volved.

As we waited for the call to come confirming a bed, the pain in Daddy's eyes and the sorrow and concern in his voice became more intense although he tried not to let it show. "Daddy, please try not to worry so much. Everything will work out fine. It's not the end of the world," I assured him.

"Well, it's nearly," he replied in a choked voice.

As the tension increased, I prayed daily for courage not to break down before my family and thus make the strain even greater. I tried to face my leave-taking realistically. I knew this was in the best interests of my mother's health. We had exhausted all other avenues. For both Daddy and Mother's sake this was the best thing to do. But I knew that there was a strong possibility—even probability—al-though no one would talk about it, that I might never see my home again. I prayed: *Oh God, just let me get out the door and past the house without going all to pieces. Help me to hold my emotions in check.*

Looking back now, I can see with better under-standing how, especially during those last few months, God had sent certain people and events into my life which helped to greatly revitalize and strengthen my sometimes faltering faith.

# THE MONSTER

Emotional trauma was no stranger to my father. I am told that there is a peculiar agony known to parents who can only stand by while their offspring suffers. Both my father and mother would willingly have exchanged their good health for the crippling paralysis which invaded my body. They had never deserted nor failed me in my hours of uncertainty and pain. Now, Daddy felt as though he was abandoning me even though he knew I would receive good care. Mother's anguish was no less real than his.

The rare and crippling disease which was to change the course of my life, and which remained undiagnosed for thirteen years, first struck in 1943 when I was a happy fun-loving seven-year-old second-grader. It paralyzed my back and arms with no warning symptoms whatsoever. One day I was practicing to be an Indian in a school play and the next I had to tell the teacher my arms wouldn't work right. I couldn't bend my back nor could I raise either arm above my head, but I could still walk normally. I had no trouble using my hands to write, hold books, and feed myself.

18

My parents took me to our doctor who was mystified. It was suggested that they take me to an orthopedic specialist.

The only symptom was a small lump at the base of my spine. My family doctor scheduled surgery to remove it. However, when I went to the hospital a week later the lump had moved all the way up my spine and down the other side, leaving my back stiff and my arms immobilized at the shoulders. Dr. Stitt immediately canceled the surgery, explaining that he had no idea what the lump was. He did not suggest any treatment.

Over the next several years, I was examined by a number of doctors in Birmingham, including orthopedic specialists. All of them were frankly mystified. One specialist, who had treated me as a baby to straighten my thumbs which had been rigidly fixed to my palms at birth, did prescribe vitamins. Little did he or any of the many others realize that my thumbs, along with my deformed big toes, were the one sure clue as to the identity of the mysterious disease.

Even though my arms and back were paralyzed from then on, my school days were no different from those of my classmates with the exception of physical education classes. I was able to participate in plays and special programs. Because I was the only child who wore glasses, I was a natural for the leading role of Old Mother Hubbard in one such program. But I did not care for the limelight and avoided it whenever possible, especially in the higher grades where oral reports were part of our assignments and the teachers asked for volunteers.

There were the usual rivalries, spats, and personality clashes common to any group of children. I do not, however, recall any incident of intentional cruelty or ridicule relating to my handicap. Many of my classmates were very considerate. They retrieved dropped pencils, got books off high shelves, and did other things they knew were difficult if not impossible for me.

In looking back, I realize I created a special problem for my teachers because often they were concerned for my health and safety. I have always been grateful that they demanded my best efforts academically and that they saw the wisdom in not pampering me or letting me get by without putting forth my very best. Along with friends I spent many recesses writing "I must not talk in class" five hundred times. I also joined classmates in sweeping floors as punishment for various infractions against the teacher's rules. I was excluded only from those games and events in which I personally chose not to participate.

I was an enthusiastic spectator at basketball games during my junior and senior years and joined my friends in yelling ourselves hoarse. My father, a fan himself, provided transportation to the games.

I had three friends whose name also began with "M," so we dubbed ourselves "The Four M's." These girls were always around to help me put on or take off my coat, fix wind-blown hair, hold water faucets, or whatever needed doing. Maggie Sue, Melba Ruth, Marlyn, and I shared the same classes and worked on the school paper together.

My first nine years were spent at Baileyton Junior High where my parents knew most of the teachers from their own school days. When I had to transfer to the larger Fairview High School five miles away, all of the teachers were strangers—but not for long. At first some of them expressed apprehension and asked what they would do if I became ill or had a seizure. Mother assured them that this would not happen. (The disease I have is not characterized by seizures.) One teacher, who later became a wonderful friend, asked why Mother wanted to keep me in school in view of the fact that I would never be able to use my education.

To their credit, these teachers without exception accepted me readily, despite concern for my well-being. I have remained in contact with many of these teachers even though most of them have long since moved away. One of them visited me regularly until her confinement to a nursing home.

I encountered no particular problems because I loved to study. I'm sure my first year typing teacher wondered what she was letting herself in for. Unable to raise my arms, I had to stand in order to reach the carriage knobs when inserting paper. I could type with both hands, but I had to lean forward to shift the carriage return with my right hand. While this cut down my score somewhat on speed tests, I was still average with the rest of the class.

Hundreds of times I have reflected with gratitude that I managed keyboard technicalities. Our typewriters were arranged in groups of three on small individual tables which were joined together forming a larger center. The teacher assigned the desks in alphabetical order and mine was between two junior boys. If my unorthodox methods bothered them, they took it well in stride. They formed the habit of waiting until I had completed the margin settings according to the teacher's instructions, and then they followed suit. Soon the group behind and to our right were engaged in whispered requests for my computations. They, in turn, politely picked up dropped erasers or pencils. In these and other ways, my classmates couldn't have been kinder or more understanding.

Someone asked if any teacher in particular contributed more to my education than another. In different ways I owe a debt of gratitude to all of them for their influence on my life. One teacher in the early grades noticed my fondness for reading and encouraged me to read above my grade level. This helped to develop a love for reading that not only made schoolwork easier and more pleasant, but proved to be a virtual lifesaver in terms of my mental sanity in the difficult years ahead.

Another teacher instilled a fascination for English and English Literature that led to their becoming my favorite subjects all through school. A high school teacher's encouragement led to my interest in writing.

I once read a book entitled *Great Teachers* in which the editor had compiled a collection of first-hand accounts written from the heart by former students to acknowledge the influence of and their profound debt to teachers who had shaped and guided their lives. The editor did not attempt to select the greatest teachers of all time, but he did look for profiles of teachers who had made significant contributions at all stages of education from the elementary to college level. Not all teachers and their students who write about them are as famous as Miss Sullivan and her blind student Helen Keller, but many are the untold stories of teachers who played an influential role in the development of great men and women. For every teacher who has ever been immortalized in print by a grateful student, there are thousands of others who are just as deserving even though they remain relatively unknown outside their own schools and sphere of influence.

I graduated from high school in 1953, missing only the last two weeks of the ninth grade due to illness related to my paralysis. I came down with German measles in the middle of final exams during my senior year and had to be sent home. The last two tests were waived, but I was not about to miss the graduation exercises which I had anticipated for so long. I still had measle spots on my legs, but I got out of bed to march up the aisle in spike heels with my sixty classmates. By coincidence, I sat by my friend Mary Ellen, the only other person in the class with whom I had gone all the way through school from first grade.

The following January, two months short of my eighteenth birthday, the paralysis struck with excruciating force first one leg and then the other in less than three months. In a matter of weeks my body was too rigid to allow me to sit upright in a wheelchair.

Then came the realization that, without doubt, God had been responsible for a teacher's challenge years before which two friends and I had accepted. Part of our fifth grade class had shared a room with the sixth grade because of a teacher shortage. The teacher had announced that anyone who would work hard enough to do both fifth and sixth grade work and who passed would be promoted to the seventh grade at the end of the term. Had I not accepted that challenge and saved one year, I could never have graduated from high school.

Perhaps that double promotion which enabled me to fulfill a cherished dream and graduate with my classmates was one of the first miracles in God's plan for my life, but it certainly was not the last. Yet just like that first miracle, their real significance and the role they were to play in fitting my puzzling and frequently frustrating circumstances together were not always apparent until much later. A monster had invaded my body. What was going to happen to me?

*To Thee, O Lord, I call; My rock,*
*do not be deaf to me, Lest, if*
*Thou be silent to me, I become*
*like those who go down to the pit.*
*Hear the voice of my supplications*
*when I cry to Thee for help, when*
*I lift up my hands toward Thy holy*
*sanctuary. (Ps. 28:1-2 NAS)*

# LIFE AS A HORIZONTAL

The first six months of my life as a horizontal—just one of the many new terms I was to learn during my initiation into the world of the severely handicapped who have their own special brand of humor—were so pain-wracked that at times I was forced to concentrate on trying literally to get through just one minute at a time—sixty seconds, second by second of agony that defies description.

Powerful painkillers taken around the clock often brought no relief and there were many sleepless nights. The dawn brought only total exhaustion for both me and my parents along with the prospect of still another rough day. The pain was like having something tied to your muscles that was ripping and tearing them apart.

Lying flat on my back, unable to move and wanting nothing so much as to toss and turn in search of relief for my tortured legs and back, I wept with pain and frustration. Many times during the long days and nights I pleaded with God, "Oh, God, I can't bear this pain. Please make it go away before I go out of my mind. And give me strength to get through it all."

Several times, when the pain became more than I could bear, I begged God to just let me die and release me from all the needless suffering. There was nothing I could do for myself. *Nothing*. I have been asked if suicide entered my thoughts. Suicidal thoughts wouldn't have done me any good. I could not so much as turn to reach for a pill. The rigidity was total with the exception of my right arm from the elbow to the fingers. I could not even turn my head.

Although I did cry out to God and beg him to let me die, God knew I wasn't ready for death. He was able to see further down the road than I, and he obviously had other plans for me although I saw only more pain and long, bleak days and nights. Tears rolled down my cheeks, but I couldn't wipe them away.

I never doubted that God was in control. I may have been only an eighteen-year-old girl, but I possessed an undying faith. The seeds of that faith had been sown many years earlier. I cannot recall ever doubting that there was a God. I had grown up in the Baileyton United Methodist Church. I became a member of that church at the age of twelve and actively participated in its youth organization until I became confined to bed. There had been no dramatic conversion such as Paul experienced on the Damascus Road. Instead, there had been a quietly developing faith, a steady but almost imperceptible assurance of strength that definitely came from outside myself.

Jesus had hung suspended on a cross—stretched out—unable to move his legs, arms, and head. The picture of him as a suffering Savior was etched into my thinking.

"Read and study," my mother urged over and over again. "There's nothing wrong with your mind. Learn something. You might find a use for it sometime, and anyway, it's good exercise. If you can't exercise your legs, you can at least exercise your brain."

Fortunately, I had inherited a love of reading and learning from her. All during my school days I had read books and magazines voraciously, often wishing for more time to read. Now I had all the time in the world. It stretched out seemingly endlessly. What was I going to do with my life and all that time? Often I asked that question. Now I began to read to fill the long hours. I read indiscriminately, devouring every book and magazine someone would place in my hand. I read everything from light-hearted trivia to serious nonfiction. Then one day, in an effort to come to grips with my predicament in a more positive and constructive way, I asked for my Bible and inspirational books.

Next to the matchless promises and assurances of hope and comfort which the Bible held out to me (and does to all who will read it and believe it), perhaps the book that was to have the deepest influence on me was Norman Vincent Peale's *The Power of Positive Thinking*. Other authors who became my bedside companions were Charles Allen, Robert Ozment, Harry Emerson Fosdick, Chester Swor, (with whom I corresponded for a time), Catherine Marshall, and many, many others.

My parents did not give up hope, however, of finding out what was wrong with me and what could be done to ease the pain. All of the doctors whom we consulted, including the outstanding orthopedic specialist in Birmingham, were completely baffled as to what the disease might be. Surgery had been considered when the disease had originally struck my back as a little girl, but this was abandoned as being too uncertain. There had never been much pain accompanying the original attacks on my back and arms. This was to change dramatically when the disease struck my legs. Even then, the only treatment ever recommended was powerful drugs which should have eased the pain, but did not.

Despite the terrific pain and the gradual loss of movement in both legs, I somehow clung desperately to the hope that, although my arms had been rendered permanently paralyzed years earlier, the mobility would return to my legs once the pain subsided. After three months of almost constant and intense pain, it finally became more intermittent.

Not only were both legs paralyzed at the hips, but one knee was frozen into a bent position and would not straighten. The right knee was immobilized into a straight position and would not bend. I could not sit in a regular wheelchair, and so I had to face up to the fact that I was permanently bedridden. Each night, my father lifted me into an adjustable lawn recliner which he had mounted on a wheelbase. (I was 5' 3" tall, and my father is a slim, erect man.) This required a considerable expenditure of effort and energy on his part since I could not help in any way. The fact that my left knee was bent into an awkward position proved to be a big asset. Because my body was so rigid, Daddy simply slipped one arm beneath my right shoulder and the other across my body and grasped my leg beneath the knee. Thus he could easily swing me into the chair much to the amazement of everybody who witnessed the technique for the first time. I looked forward to the evenings when he could come in from the fields and I would be moved into the living room. I could sit comfortably for three or four hours at a time.

We prayed for healing. I had a lot of growing to do in the ways of the Lord and my spiritual discernment was sadly lacking. When God did not immediately answer my prayers for healing, I wondered if it was because I didn't have enough faith. But didn't the Bible say, "If ye have faith as a grain of mustard seed, ye shall say unto this mountain, Remove hence to yonder place; and it shall remove; and nothing shall be impossible unto you" (Matt. 17:20). Surely, surely, I reflected in agonizing soul-searching, I had *that much* faith. I began to see that Jesus was speaking of a quality not a quantity of faith. But even that was not the sole criteria for healing. My faith was to grow in quality *and* quantity. There were many lessons ahead for me which God as private Tutor would slowly reveal.

I believed completely in the Bible in those early days of being a horizontal, and I still believe in it that way. Long years of lying immobile in my hospital bed at home have not diminished my faith in the God of the impossible. I saw Jesus performing miraculous healings while he was here on earth; I believe that he can perform and is performing those same healing miracles on earth today.

The Bible tells us to ask and believe and "ye shall receive." That is presented as a running theme throughout the Word of God in such places as Matthew 21:22, Mark 11:24, John 16:23, and elsewhere. I read those promises over and over again in my desperate struggle to find some key or clue which would reveal the "secret" and make them work for me. I read Psalm 37:5, "Commit thy way unto the Lord; trust also in him; and *he shall bring it to pass,*" and knew that my commitment and my trust were not lacking.

In the fifth chapter of John, I discovered the story of the man beside the pool of whom Jesus asked, "Wilt thou be made whole?" (v. 6). When the man, who had been lame for thirty-eight years, complained that he had no one to lift him into the water, Jesus commanded him simply, "Rise, take up thy bed, and walk" (v. 8). The Bible tells us that the man did exactly that.

But my own fervent and heartfelt, "Yes, Lord, make *me* whole," did not restore *my* physical wholeness. At this point in my immature faith it would have been so easy to have given up in despair—to have cursed God in discouragement and bitterness and to have died as Job's friends urged him to do.

One day, while reading a magazine article, I came across a quotation by Harry Emerson Fosdick that seemed to leap from the pages straight at me and stick in my mind. It read: "You can't live better by living bitter."

Something inside me seemed to be saying that there in a nutshell was a clear-cut choice for the course of my life. I was at a crossroads, and the decision was mine alone to make. The route I chose would determine to an even greater extent than my physical limitations whether I defeated—or was defeated by—the vicious monster that had invaded my body.

Bitter or better. God spoke to me in a way that I have since come to recognize as a still small inner voice which can be relied upon. That day he said, "Margaret Jean, you can bemoan your fate, wallow in misery and self-pity, or you can start searching for constructive ways to add meaning to the life I have given you."

Be strong and of a good
courage. (Josh. 1:6)

# BITTER OR BETTER?

I once read that in acceptance lieth peace. I did not
ask of my parents "Why? Why me?" Somehow God
gave me the wisdom to know that by complaining and
questioning I would only add to their already
burdened and sad hearts. I saw my friends go off to
college, others got married and moved away. Friends
and relatives continued to call and stop by to visit.
God also spared me from having envious feelings
toward others. There was nothing to be gained from
mournful introspection and dreaming about what
might have been. I didn't want to become depressed
and was spared deep depression. I know now that this
was all of God. I didn't possess the inner reservoir of
an all-sufficient faith to buoy me through the pain
and uncertainty. A high price is paid for growth, and
it doesn't happen overnight.

It is not difficult to take the "yes" answers to our
prayers and pleadings, and the "no" answers can
even be accepted with a measure of good grace; it is
the waiting that is hardest. Days follow days and the
temptation exists to question God. Although I would

not impose upon my parents the burden of my
unanswered questions, nevertheless in the darkness
of the night, when sleep would not come and
unbidden tears filled my eyes, I conversed with God
and sought answers.

God's answers sometimes come in unexpected
ways. He knows us better than we know ourselves.
He knew that deep inside, Margaret Jean Jones
would never be satisfied until she at least knew what
the disease was and that every means for help had
been exhausted.

It was about this time that a dear friend brought
me a copy of the *Saturday Evening Post* with the
suggestion that I might be interested in a certain
article it contained. The article concerned the great
strides medical research was making at the National
Institute of Health (NIH) in Bethesda, Maryland.
Supported by the United States government, this
giant clinical research center concentrates on diseases for which there is no known cure. Patient
eligibility is restricted to certain types of several
specific diseases such as cancer, heart disease,
kidney disease, arthritis, and nerve disorders.
Patients with "the disease of the month" are
admitted with the understanding that they will be
serving as human guinea pigs, participating in
experimental-type treatments that have previously
been extensively tested only on laboratory animals.

One of the primary requirements for admission to
NIH is that the patient's disease have a confirmed
diagnosis. Mine wasn't, despite the fact that by this
time I had been afflicted with it for more than
thirteen years. During this time I had been examined
by numerous doctors and had been under the care of a

noted specialist until the age of fifteen. All of them had made numerous X-rays but none, with the exception of my family physician who had originally scheduled surgery and changed his mind at the last moment, had ever suggested any type treatment or therapy.

The article incited my interest. It reported the successful treatment of case histories which had previously been considered hopeless. This caused me to wonder if perhaps one of the doctors on the NIH medical team which was made up of some of the best doctors in the nation might have a diagnosis of my disease and also some type of treatment for it.

I became convinced that if there was a medical solution or if one could be found, those researchers at NIH would know about it. I determined to try for admission despite the lack of diagnosis. But first I had to overcome the objections of my parents and, in fact, my whole family, none of whom could bear the thought of my being alone in a hospital eight hundred miles from home.

I was now twenty years old and had never stayed away from home before. No one but Mother had ever nursed me. There were certain procedures pertaining to my personal care that we had worked out only after much trial and error and no little frustration. For instance, my clothes could be gotten on in only one way and it had to be exact. If situated in a certain position I could sit comfortably in bed for several hours without adjustment. Any variation on that "just right" position and I become uncomfortable in a matter of minutes. Some of these innovations were custom-designed to fit my particular needs. Some of them were in direct conflict to things taught in nursing manuals. (Mother had borrowed one from an RN friend in an effort to learn how to properly care for me.) Mother worried that the nurses at NIH might not understand or want to try our techniques, and she was afraid I would be continually uncomfortable.

I knew that my parents could neither afford the expense nor the time away from farming to stay with me. But even before I realized what I might need, God gave me inner strength and assurance that I could stay by myself for however long was necessary. I knew my prayers were being answered. Psalm 18 became a great source of encouragement to me.

1 I will love thee, O Lord, my strength.
2 The Lord is my rock, and my fortress,
   and my deliverer; my God, my strength,
   in whom I will trust; my buckler, and
   the horn of my salvation, and my high
   tower.
3 I will call upon the Lord, who is worthy
   to be praised: so shall I be saved from
   mine enemies.

The disease was my enemy—vicious and cruel.

6 In my distress I called upon the Lord,
   and cried unto my God: he heard my voice
   out of his temple, and my cry came before
   him, even unto his ears.
26 With the pure thou wilt shew thyself pure. . . .
28 For thou wilt light my candle: the Lord my
   God will enlighten my darkness.
30 As for God, his way is perfect: the
   word of the Lord is tried; he is a
   buckler to all those that trust in
   him.

31 For who is God save the Lord? or who
   is a rock save our God?
39 For thou hast girded me with strength
   unto the battle. . . .

I listened to my parents voice their concern, but
inside I knew that at NIH there were answers and
that the article that had been given to me had not
been given by accident.

"What if they try some kind of experiment that
makes you worse instead of better?" Daddy asked
anxiously.

I wanted to say, "What could be worse than just
lying here rigid like this?" but I remained silent.

"What if they want to do a series of operations, and
we can't be with you?" Mother worried. We thought
about these concerns for awhile. But only a short
while, for even greater than their natural anxieties
was a desire that I walk again, and they could see and
sense how much I wanted to do this. They didn't want
to leave any stone unturned that might contribute to
my improvement. I understood their reluctance to let
me try and turn "the stones" alone among complete
strangers in an, as yet, unknown method. Like me,
my parents believed that God would always sustain
me in whatever experience lay ahead. In the end, I
successfully convinced them that I really wanted to
go and that I would be all right, and finally, they
agreed to let me try for admittance.

We knew there was only a very slim chance that
the clinic would accept me as a patient. In the first
place, there were scores of applications for each
available bed. Secondly, there was the problem of no

diagnosis. But it was certainly worth a try. "Mother and Daddy," I said, "there's absolutely nothing to lose by trying."

With that statement Mother herself carried the magazine article to Dr. Stitt, our family physician, and told him how anxious I was to know if NIH knew anything about my disease. The article stated that all applications had to be recommended by a doctor.

Over the years, Dr. Stitt had treated almost every member of the Jones family. I have only one brother, but there were fourteen aunts and uncles with their tribes of children, and we all claimed him as our doctor. We laughed when he instructed a nurse who expressed concern over the large number waiting anxiously outside the patient's door not to worry. "That's only part of them. The rest will be here shortly. Just let them all in," he was heard to say. Another time, we were deeply touched as we glimpsed the sadness that swept across his face when he abruptly turned away from a question asked by a terminally ill relative whom he had treated for nearly thirteen years.

Dr. Stitt walked tall both in the eyes of the medical profession, where he was regarded with respect, and in the life of the community, where he participated generously and was dear in the hearts of his friends and patients to whom he was dedicated to serve.

I knew, too, that Dr. Stitt was a talented servant of mankind who walked humbly with God, unafraid to admit his frailties, unashamed to reveal his dependence upon a higher Power and to suggest that Source to his patients. I respected, admired, and loved him very much, not only for his medical skill, but for his interest and concern for my life as a whole.

Often his words of encouragement helped me to cope with the problems for which he was unable to find a medical solution.

When mother went to Dr. Stitt with the magazine and my request, he quickly agreed to send a complete resume of my case history as he knew it to one of the doctors mentioned in the article. He also sent X-rays that had been made at various times as the disease had progressed. He then cautioned us not to get our hopes up because his letter was, at best, only a stab in the dark and the odds were high that nobody at NIH would even bother to answer it.

After six months had elapsed and we received no answer, we asked Dr. Stitt to send a follow-up letter. He wasted no time in doing so, and a short time later he received a request from Dr. Frederick Bartter, head of the National Heart Institute, asking to see more of my X-rays.

Just before Christmas of 1956, Dr. Stitt received a second letter from Dr. Bartter stating a tentative diagnosis of myositis ossificans progressiva. This was the first diagnosis ever offered by anyone. I was overwhelmed. Surely this in itself was an answer to my prayers. Now we could at least call the disease by name.

The letter also stated that a group of doctors at the clinic, including Dr. Bartter, were very interested in studying the case further because it was extremely rare. I was being accepted as a patient and could be admitted at my earliest convenience.

It was a great Christmas present for me, and there was an air of excitement when the Jones clan gathered at my grandparents' house on Christmas day. We made train reservations for January 7, 1957 and sent an airmail letter to NIH advising them of the date and time of our arrival. Following instructions in their letter, we requested they have an ambulance to meet us at Union Station in Washington, D.C.

On the Sunday before we were due to leave, two of our closest friends, without our knowledge, went out among friends and neighbors in our small rural community and collected enough money to pay my train fare. When they came and presented me with more than three hundred dollars as a token of their love and support, I was overwhelmed with emotion. Tears flowed as I read the names of these kind and generous people who wanted to share in the fight with disease.

In the weeks ahead these same friends sent cards and letters almost daily to help ward off the loneliness they knew I was experiencing. Friends, I am convinced, are among life's greatest blessings. My life has been immeasurably enriched because of the acts of love and deeds of kindness which I have so often received at their hands. Through the years, I have never ceased to be amazed at these same friends, along with new friends and strangers alike, who have come into my life always at just the moment I needed them most. They have added a dimension to my life that could come in no other way.

We prayed for a safe journey, and before we reached our destination God answered that prayer in a way so startling that we knew God was watching over us. We left Birmingham in the late afternoon and were due to arrive in Washington the following morning around eight. When we reached Atlanta the train was delayed for over an hour. The porter came to tell us he had asked the dispatcher to call ahead and notify the clinic of our new arrival time. A few minutes later the porter was back to inform us that NIH knew nothing about our impending arrival. The airmail letter we had mailed ten days earlier had not been received.

The "lost" letter arrived on Dr. Bartter's desk several hours after I had been comfortably settled in a seventh-floor room. The chief himself made a special trip to my room to show it to me.

The knowledge of how close we came to arriving at the bustling Union Station in Washington with no ambulance waiting sent shivers down our spines. But the tangible knowledge of God's intervention in what could have been a long and painful wait in a strange city and in such a busy place, made me even more keenly aware that God always sees around the next curve and through the tunnels long before we do. He can be counted upon to see us safely through. When you have placed yourself in God's hands, you will not be stranded or forsaken.

Weeks of emotionally trying and often painful experimental treatments were to follow. I remembered God's words to Moses' successor, Joshua, when he was told, "Be strong and of a good courage" (1:6), and I repeated them to myself over and over again. This verse became a deeply personal challenge. But I knew where my strength was coming from—it was surely not anything I possessed in and of myself. God could be depended upon to provide for my needs.

*He giveth power to the faint;*
*and to them that hath no might*
*he increaseth strength. (Isa. 40:29)*

## HIGH HOPES

I had vivid dreams of walking again—visions of ordinary things that most people take for granted, like walking into stores or down the church aisle—and I thought walking off a plane would be terribly exciting. I had several dreams where I was, in fact, walking from a plane. I entered the National Institute of Health in Bethesda, Maryland, with high hopes on January 8, 1957. I was to spend the next eighteen weeks there.

After X-rays of every bone in my body from head to toe (and from every angle), along with other tests, I was placed on a metabolic diet and cortisone medication, which was then still in experimental stages. A metabolic diet, I learned, meant that you chose from a prepared list as much and as many different foods as you desired for three daily meals, plus snacks if you wanted them. You were required to eat exactly the same food right down to the very last crumb and drop every day for as long as the doctor ordered.

Several patients, including one who had already

41

been on a salt-free diet for six months, kindly warned of the monotony and cautioned me to choose small portions because all of it would become detestable sooner or later. Much to my amusement, I soon learned that they were not exaggerating when the dietician did indeed bring back my place and order me to swallow tiny crumbs under her watchful eyes. This happened more than once.

All body wastes were collected and carefully measured on a round-the-clock basis. We were also weighed at precisely the same time each morning in a hospital-furnished robe. Patients were forbidden to go on the sun deck because the fresh air might cause variations in the precisely measured tests.

In addition to the metabolic diet and cortisone experiment, it was also decided to try a series of operations in an effort to unlock the stiffness in my joints and restore movement to my arms and legs. Dr. Bartter kindly explained what they planned to do during surgery and gave me a choice as to where I wanted to begin. I chose to start with my arms. If that proved successful they would then follow the same procedures on my hips.

While at NIH I had the pleasure of becoming acquainted with a remarkable group of young men and women between the ages of eighteen and twenty-five who were quietly performing an invaluable service for medical science in order that all mankind might benefit. These perfectly healthy young people were known to the staff and patients alike as "Normal Controls." Most of them were members of the Church of the Brethren, along with a few Mennonites. Many were just out of high school. Some had one or more years of college. A few were

college graduates. All of them were devout Christians who were tithing a part of their lives for the
glory of God and in service to their fellowman.

I learned that some of them had already spent time
on the mission field in the United States and South
America in various teaching, preaching, and labor-
ing capacities before coming to NIH. At the clinic
these "Normal Controls" would serve six months to a
year or longer as human guinea pigs, lending their
healthy bodies and participating in experiments
made by the scientists that might one day lead to
better diagnosis, treatment, and prevention of major
illnesses. They were sometimes paired with a specific
patient. Each was put on a metabolic diet and given
the same dosage of a certain drug. Then the reaction
of the drug in the healthy body was compared with
that of someone with cancer, heart disease, arthritis,
kidney ailments, mental illness, dental infections,
neurological disorders, and other disabilities.

No experiment was ever conducted which could
permanently damage a Normal's health, nevertheless many of the experiments caused much discom-
fort and inconvenience, such as being dehydrated for
a short time, taking an injection (to study mental
illness), being deprived of sleep, or being isolated in a
sealed chamber where every breath and heartbeat
was recorded. The "Nomal Controls" were serious in
their dedication, but also full of life and fun. They
were a great morale booster to all the patients and a
tremendous inspiration to me.

There were three girls in the "Normal Control"
group on my wing. Through them I became acquainted with others. They dropped by my room
several times daily bringing sunshine and inspira-

tion through their dedication and wonderful example of faith. They offered to do small chores for me, and one girl volunteered to set my hair in pincurls every few days. They also pushed my wheelchair to the chapel on the fourteenth floor each Sunday morning. In addition, they saw to it that I got to the movies and other entertainment programs throughout the week.

The first Sunday I was there, a girl named Eleanor Stamper from Johnstown, Pennsylvania, took me to church. Dr. Edward Bigelieri, a handsome Italian whom I was to come to know and respect very much in the weeks ahead, assisted the nurses in lifting me into the chair.

That first Sunday I attended church was an overwhelming experience in more ways than one. Actually, it marked the first time I had been out in public among a group of people since becoming paralyzed three years before. As a matter of fact, I hadn't even been outside my home until I started on the trip to NIH. I felt very timid and self-conscious.

The fact that my wheelchair was a special lounge-type model, which had been languishing in the storage room because they hadn't had a use for it in many years, didn't help matters much. It stood out like a Ford station wagon in a carlot full of Cadillacs.

Despite my self-consciousness, I couldn't help being excited about attending church for the first time in three years. The large chapel was lovely with stained-glass windows along the outside wall, red carpet, a beautiful organ, and a large cross behind the simply furnished altar. The altar was surrounded by a gleaming wooden rail and a low kneeling bench. I learned later that the altar was specially constructed on a revolving base so that it could be used for Protestant, Catholic, and Jewish worship services.

The chapel was crowded with white and black patients, doctors, nurses, technicians, dieticians, and maids and orderlies, sitting side by side in worshipful silence. The order of worship was simple and traditional. As I joined the congregation in singing familiar old hymns, and as I listened to the chaplain deliver an inspiring message of hope, I thought of my own family and friends back in our little rural Methodist church at Baileyton, Alabama. I knew that even then they were praying for me even as I prayed for them. My heart tingled as I felt God's amazing power communicate love and thoughts across the many hundreds of miles that separated us.

At the end of the service, many of this congregation, whose faces were to become so familiar over the next few months (although I never learned all their names), smiled warmly at me or spoke a word of greeting. At the door, the chaplain greeted each one with a handshake, a word of welcome, and a soft "God bless you." Their spirits renewed, the patients walked or rolled away prepared to face another week of tests, pain, and waiting.

*Is anyone among you suffering? He should keep on praying about it. (James 5:13 TLB)*

# EXHIBIT "A" IN A BIKINI

We can joke about it now, but at the time it wasn't exactly funny. Of the more than two dozen doctors who examined me personally, and the scores of others at a weekly medical conference at which I was exhibit "A" (in a bikini with about three dozen X-rays strung up behind me), none had ever seen a case like mine except Dr. Bartter who made the original diagnosis. Following extensive X-rays and tests, it was decided to perform surgery on the front and back of my arms at the shoulder in an attempt to increase the range of motion. Considerable bone, which studies later showed to be normal, was removed from my right shoulder including bony bridges that connect the humerus to the scapula and chest cage. The operations were two weeks apart. Following the second operation I was able to raise my arm high enough to touch my eye with my index finger. The doctors were hopeful, and so was I.

Our elation was short-lived, however. The increased range of motion lasted for only a matter of days. Even with extensive physiotherapy, my arm

46

soon became fixed again, this time with more abduction than before.

No range of motion was ever gained as a result of the operations on my left arm. New bone formation occurred at an extremely rapid rate. X-rays revealed new bone two or three weeks after the operation.

For ten weeks following the first operation, I was placed on a combination of steroids. The clinical response was uniformly poor. The return of immobilization seemed to be in no way delayed or prevented by the steroid medication. The doctors determined that my propensity to grow new bone was tremendous.

Before each operation I prayed that God would make the surgery successful so that I could use my arms normally. Before one of my operations, one of the team doctors, a lovely Filipino lady who came around with Dr. Bartter each Monday, leaned down and gently touched me on the shoulder.

"Margaret, we will be watching the operation tomorrow, and we will be praying for you," she said softly.

I knew that many of my new "Normal Control" friends were praying also in the chapel while I was in the operating room. And I knew too that relatives and friends in Cullman and elsewhere were earnestly praying.

As the time for each operation drew near, I felt very close to God, and I knew that he was going to be in that operating room. Even after suffering an excruciatingly painful attack on my left arm shortly after the fourth operation, which resulted in further loss of its already severely limited motion, I remained hopeful.

It has only been in more recent years, with the help of my doctors in Cullman, that I have been able to obtain a bibliography of some of the papers that have been written about research on the disease. Dr. Morris asked that I choose what appeared to be the most interesting titles in light of my personal experience. He then had these articles photostated and sent to me. It was also about this time that a friend introduced me to a registered nurse from southern California who had access to a large medical library. She, too, sent me another bibliography and a copy of an article describing the symptoms of the disease.

And so it was that after playing host to this disease for thirty-five years, I was finally able to read what is actually known about it. According to the description of symptoms, mine was a classic case, deviating little from the onset, progression, and effects as noted by various researchers.

It came as no surprise to discover that the disease is considered extremely rare. The condition was first noted by Guy Patin in 1692 who described the case as "the woman who turned to wood." For aptness, you can take it from this writer that the description cannot be improved upon. A doctor once told my mother that some people with the disease have traveled with the circus as "petrified humans."

It was nearly two hundred years later that a man by the name of Von Dusch first used the name myositis ossificans progressiva; and in 1869 it became known as Munchmeyer's Disease after the man who gave the first comprehensive report on the disease with an account of twelve cases. Today, some doctors favor fibrodysplasia ossificans progressiva as a more apt medical definition.

By whatever name it is called, the exact cause is still unknown. It has been largely concluded that the basic pathogenetic factor appears to be a hereditary defect of some element of connective tissue between muscles so that there is a proliferation of the interstitial tissue between muscles, followed by calcification and bone formation.

And, regardless of what it is called, I have to agree with the writer in a medical journal who said "Myositis ossificans is so terrible and so rare a disease, that the results of reasonable efforts to treat it should be published."

Onset of the disease is usually in the first ten years, and it rarely begins after the age of twenty. According to one doctor, there were one hundred eighteen known cases worldwide in 1918. Over the years, a wide variety of treatments have been tried ranging from local bleeding, sarsaparilla, and low calcium diets, to ultrasound and surgical removal of ectopic bone, all with no success. In recent years, experiments with sodium etidronate (EHDP) have resulted in the restoration of some movement in the immobilized muscles of a few victims, while in others there was no improvement at all.

I was particularly struck by three of the findings, all of which came as a total surprise. The first was that the disease seems to be more prevalent among males, possibly by as much as four to one according to one researcher. Secondly, it seems to be generally agreed that the disease is hereditary. As a genealogy buff who has extensive contact with various branches on both sides of my family, I have never found any evidence of a relative with a condition that remotely resembles it.

But, to me, the most outstanding discovery was the fact that all known victims have one thing in common: short big toes which are missing the second joint and curve inward toward the second toe to form a sort of wedge shape. About 50 percent of the cases also have short thumbs (which I have).

One of the articles mentions the fact that only very rarely does a doctor initially examining a patient with these abnormalities recognize them as being sure clues.

At no time had any of the doctors who examined me ever mentioned the connection of my short toes and thumbs with the disease. Nor have I ever read an article in a popular magazine or newspaper medical column that has mentioned the disease and its symptoms in any way.

Even before I was aware of these discoveries, Dr. Morris had strongly urged me to write my experience for a medical journal. I thought about that and then began to realize that after a silence of thirty-five years, it was more than mere coincidence that I should acquire the knowledge I now have to write a book in which the disease plays a prominent role.

We know more about the disease now than we have ever known at any point hitherto, and I am continuing my search in medical journals. But regardless of any present or future findings, I have accepted the fact that God has entrusted me with this disease. In *The Living Bible,* James 5, I have found that which speaks to me, for I have often identified with the biblical Job in his sufferings.

For examples of patience in suffering, look at the Lord's prophets. We know how happy they are now because they stayed true to him then, even though they suffered greatly for it. Job is an example of a man who continued to trust the Lord in sorrow; from his experiences we can see how the Lord's plan finally ended in good, for he is full of tenderness and mercy. (vv. 10, 11)

*My brothers, you will always have your trials but, when they come, try to treat them as a happy privilege; you understand that your faith is only put to the test to make you patient, but patience too is to have its practical results so that you will become fully developed, complete, with nothing missing. (James 1:2-4 TJB)*

# BIRTHDAY BOULEVARD

"Happy birthday to you, happy birthday to you,
Happy birthday, dear Margaret, happy birthday to you."

I looked up at the singers from my hospital bed and had to smile. There they stood with a plate of toast and a flickering candle perched atop. It was my twenty-first birthday, and I was celebrating it at NIH.

When you are twenty-one, patience is far down the list of priorities. James, chapter one, speaks of our faith as being put to the test so as to develop our patience. *The Amplified Bible* says to "Consider it wholly joyful, my brethren, whenever you are enveloped in or encounter trials of any sort . . . Be assured and understand that the trial and proving of your faith bring out endurance and steadfastness and patience" (James 1:2, 3).

As I lay there reflecting on the fact that I had reached another birthday milestone, I thought about the many paths waiting to be explored, the many challenges beckoning, the many dreams to be fulfilled. I did not possess enough mature insight to see that sometimes God purchases us a ticket on a ferryboat plying stormy seas rather than on a supersonic jet sailing smoothly through clear skies.

The paralysis of my body did not inhibit the dreams, fantasies, and natural desires that flash vividly and urgently—and often unbidden and unexpectedly—through a healthy and active mind. For, contrary to what I was to learn is a misconception shared by far too many people, malfunctioning muscles do not automatically mean the mind is immobilized too. Or at least it should not be.

When God's ferryboat leaves you marooned on a tiny bed-sized island with meager resources with which to plot a rescue, patience begins to command more respect. That doesn't mean it becomes an overnight acquisition, or automatic endowment. The assumption made by many people that the severely handicapped possess a secret formula or a magic supply of patience and courage is as much a myth as the assumption that physical impairment automatically means there are also mental handicaps involved.

Nothing could be further from the truth. Patience can be just as elusive, wear just as thin, snap just as easily on a lonesome, seemingly aimless journey, with only one's thoughts for companionship and no particular time schedule, as it can at a busy intersection where all roads hint at exciting adventure, and there is an urgent desire to explore them all. Nor does courage spring full-blown like a sudden burst of adrenalin in the face of great adversity. Before the seeds of either can take root and grow, we must set ourselves the task of cleaning away the

weeds and underbrush of self-pity, despair, and
bitterness.

How did I do it? It took time. I'm still working at it.
The book of Hebrews tells us that the God of
peace—who is the Author and Giver of peace—pro-
vides what is lacking in our lives when we submit to
him. It says that he strengthens (completes and
perfects) and makes us what we ought to be and
equips us with everything good that we may carry
out his will while he himself works in us. Thus he
accomplishes that which is pleasing in his sight, and
it all comes about through Jesus (see Heb. 13:21
TAB).

My mother relates that one day, many years ago,
while she was washing dishes and feeling sorry for
herself, the Lord clearly spoke to her and said, "Mrs.
Jones, perhaps you are a privileged person." Mother
shared this with me one day when I was having a
pity-party. I tried to keep such times from her, but
mothers are sensitive, and mine is especially so. She
knew. And I began to think that perhaps I, too, was a
privileged person.

I didn't think so that day in mid-May, shortly after
my twenty-first birthday, when Dr. Bigelieri unexpectedly announced that I could be dismissed as soon
as my parents could make arrangements to come for
me. "The surgery, Margaret, thus far has failed and
all of us are reluctant to try more on your hips at this
time. We simply don't know of any other medical
treatment to try. We are going to keep the case on
active file and if we can come up with some type of
treatment, we will call you back for readmittance
later. I'm so sorry we were unable to help you," he
told me gently.

The call never came. Sometimes, I still had vivid dreams in which I was walking normally and doing the things I longed to do. On awaking, I could recall every detail of these dreams. I wasn't depressed over them but I often wondered if, indeed, they had any real significance.

All hopes of a medical solution to my physical problems died with the failure at NIH. But at least now we knew. I felt that my earlier prayers had been answered—oh, not in the way I had hoped, to be sure, but I knew that God knew what he was up to. I told my parents I knew there was no longer any point in running up huge doctor bills and plunging them deeper into debt by going from specialist to specialist only to have them shake their heads in bewilderment and mumble "sorry." I knew my father would have gladly made any sacrifice had we been given any encouragement.

Except for powerful pain-relievers taken during the height of severely painful paralytic attacks, that continued to occur at intervals ranging from three months to as long as seven years apart, my hospitalization at NIH was to mark the last time that I sought examination or treatment specifically for the myositis ossificans condition.

Some years later, in writing about past birthday milestones on Birthday Boulevard, I recalled my twenty-first birthday. Like the scenes along the concrete highways crisscrossing the land, Birthday Boulevard has its own memorable scenes in the traveler's life. Some are recalled with amusement, others with nostalgia; some with pride, and others with pain; some with happiness, others through a flood of tears. Some we would just as soon forget and others we would cling to forever.

Mishaps and detours also occur on Birthday Boulevard which often leave tragedy and heartbreak in their wake. We break the laws of responsible action and suffer progressive paralysis in the future. We fail to negotiate the curve of diappointment and plunge into an abyss of despair. We crash head-on into failure and receive a crushed spirit.

We violate health rules and become ill. We disregard moral standards and sustain degenerative injuries to our reputation and character. We ignore religious teachings and invite spiritual death. We fail to heed the signs, and as we near the end of our journey we are apt to discover, too late, that we missed out on many wonderful experiences that might have been ours.

The traveler on Birthday Boulevard never knows when his journey will end. It might be abruptly at the top of the next hill or many milestones later. The number on those milestones does not matter nearly so much as the fact that we have been privileged to reach another. Numbers alone are meaningless. It's the enjoyment and appreciation of the scenery along the way that counts.

None of us has the assurance of another tomorrow. I know that my chances of longevity are considerably less than the normally healthy person. It has been shown that ossification is uncommon in the smaller muscles and in those of the abdomen. The heart, diaphragm, larynx, tongue, sphincter, and eye muscles are usually not involved. I have learned, however, that death in many cases has come from respiratory disease or from ossification of the masseter muscles (the large muscles in the angle of the lower jaw, which raise the jaw in chewing) resulting in starvation.

But I do not fear this. I am looking forward to going to heaven. And why not? Heaven is the reward of the righteous and the faithful; heaven is the dwelling place of God and his Son, my Savior. And there I will walk again.

*For now we see through a glass*
*[in a mirror], darkly; but then*
*face to face: now I know in part;*
*but then shall I know even as*
*also I am known. (I Cor. 13:12)*

# THROUGH THE LOOKING GLASS

After I returned home from NIH, I settled into a daily routine of reading, gazing out the window by holding a little hand mirror (because I couldn't turn my head), watching television (at night when Daddy would lift me into the specially built chair and roll me into the living room), and reading some more.

My cousin Sharron, who was three years younger than I and lived next door, came to visit me every afternoon after school for four years until she graduated. My own friends had gone away to college or married, but Sharron and my brother Bob often brought their friends to visit. These lively teen-agers kept me well entertained.

By this time, my brother Bob was attending St. Bernard College in Cullman as a commuting student. Without too much trouble, he cajoled me into helping him with some of his special assignments after he designed and constructed a bookrack to hold the heavy text and reference books. My father might have gotten a bargain by getting two college educations for the price of one, except that I didn't see

58

any future need for a degree in Business Administration. Appropriateness aside, on the night of his graduation Bob and a friend hatched up a scheme to make me a graduate too. At the end of the graduation exercises in the football stadium, Bob, still wearing his cap and gown, came around to where I was sitting in front of the bleachers. Before I realized what he was up to, he took off his mortarboard and placed it on my head. A friend was standing by to snap my startled expression as the spectators around us burst into applause and laughter.

Relatives and family friends continued to visit me often. Sometimes they would bring their own friends whom I had never met. Thus I became acquainted with many interesting people from all walks of life and formed many meaningful new friendships. Out of curiosity, I kept a guest book for two or three years and found that I had more than five hundred visitors a year. It has been the thoughtfulness of these many people through the years which has done so much to encourage and challenge me to keep an active interest in what is going on about me and in the world at large and given me a searching mind and a hopeful spirit.

The late great Helen Keller, a world-famous author and lecturer who was universally admired for her courage in overcoming multiple handicaps, once declared: "Sick or well, blind or seeing, bond or free, we are all here for a purpose and however we are situated, we please God better with useful deeds than with many prayers of pious resignation."

I don't think anyone who has ever sought to overcome thwarted ambitions or pick up the pieces of shattered dreams can dispute the truth of those words. Nor can they remain unmoved by the challenging example set by this remarkable woman who was deprived of both sight and hearing at the age of three. At the same time, there is the matter of often having to come to grips with another truth: one of the largest of those "useful deeds" Miss Keller spoke of just might be a willingness to turn resignation into acceptance.

According to Webster, resignation means to submit or give up deliberately. Acceptance is to receive or take willingly. Where rehabilitation is concerned, whether physical, mental, emotional, or spiritual, learning—and more importantly experiencing—the difference is likened to walking out of a dark tunnel into a sun-dappled meadow.

All too often, I think, we tend to congratulate ourselves for having achieved acceptance of a situation that we cannot change when, in reality, we are merely resigned to it. Too frequently, perhaps, we are not even aware of the difference between acceptance and resignation until we wake up one day to find that the impassive attitude of simply apathetically making the best of a situation is not too much of an improvement over the original feelings of frustration and despair. What is needed is the cultivation of that tiny spark of perseverance which God plants within each of us, and then fanning it into a burning desire to make the most of any given situation regardless of the circumstances.

Charles Spurgeon, the famous nineteenth-century English theologian, once wrote that one should

Cry for grace from God to be able to see His hand in every trial and then for grace to submit at once to it.

Not only to submit, but to acquiesce and to rejoice in it.
I think there is generally an end to trouble when we
reach this point.

As I sought this grace, sometimes from atop a
tower of optimism, and sometimes from amid the
rubble of bulldozed ideas, I gradually came to realize
with the profundity that can only come from deep
personal experience, that genuine happiness—that
sense of abiding joy that lingers and grows richer,
rather than momentary pleasures that waver and
dissipate—depends not so much on the fate that
dictates our lives as on our attitude toward that
dictation.

Although God is the Architect for the blueprints of
our lives, and the supreme Superintendent of
whatever is built, he still expects us to pour the
cement, lay the bricks, and hammer the boards in
place—even if we do get a few smashed fingers in our
bumbling ineptitude.

Sometimes, he sends a rather odd-looking hodge-
podge of seemingly unrelated raw materials and
challenges us to make something beautiful for him. If
we are surprised at the outcome, we shouldn't be,
because the apostle Paul tells us that "God has given
each of us the ability to do certain things well" (Rom.
12:6 TLB). God is also the perfect Instructor who
teaches us to see a lovely rock garden where before
we had seen only an ugly old rock pile.

I know a creative lady who deliberately seeks the
challenge of making something lovely using nothing
but castoffs from the trash heap. One day, while
peeling potatoes for lunch, she hit on the idea of
fashioning flowers from oven-dried potato peels.

Colored with acryllic paints, the unusual bouquet became quite a conversation piece.

Likewise, difficulties and trials can become interesting and exciting adventures. When we follow God's roadmap he often leads us along routes that we would never have chosen but which afford experiences "exceeding abundantly above all that we ask or think, according to the power that worketh in us" (Eph. 3:20).

In 1960, I suffered a severe attack of myositis ossificans on my jaws with dire consequences. They became frozen so tightly that less than half a peanut could be wedged between my upper and lower molars. The pain was almost unbearable and pain-killers did not help. Through necessity, my diet was greatly restricted. My favorite foods, fruitcake and corn-on-the-cob, were gone forever. Unfortunately, it was December, and mother had just baked some delicious fruitcakes. I could, however, still manage many foods if they were chopped finely enough.

This problem was compounded ten years later when a second major attack closed my jaws completely. Now, I could eat only foods that were blended perfectly smooth. The fact that this occurred during the writing of my first history book was a lifesaver because I was too busy to dwell on the intense pain or what I could no longer eat.

God had not chosen to heal my paralysis and restore me to the regular mainstream of independence. But neither had he erected a sign at the washed-out bridge I had encountered on his roadmap informing me to just lie there and wait until the river dried up so that I could cross without difficulty.

I recalled the parable Jesus told his disciples about

the servant who hid the one talent given him by his master rather than trying to multiply it like the servant who had been given five talents and the other who had been given two. When the master returned and called his servants to account, he rebuked the servant who had hidden his talent in the ground. The talent was taken from him and given to the servant who had proved himself faithful. And the master said, "For unto every one that hath shall be given, and he shall have abundance: but from him that hath not shall be taken away even that which he hath" (Matt. 25:29).

The message was clear to me. A willingness to try—not necessarily for superior performance—effort, not spectacular success, is what God asks of us in return for his priceless gift of love and life.

An unknown Trappist monk in the Abbey of Genesee expressed this magnificently when he wrote:

> God has given me this day to use as I will. I can waste it or use it for good. What I do today is important because I am exchanging a day of my life for it. When tomorrow comes, the day will be gone forever, leaving in its place something I have traded for it. I want it to be gain, not loss; good, not evil; success, not failure; in order that I shall not regret the price I paid for it.

I became convinced that simply to idle the time away with no service to others or self-improvement was not only a fast and sure way of losing one's grip on reality, but also would be a dishonor to God.

A prominent psychologist once wrote that all of us have at least a thousand talents. Most of them, he said, remain latent all our lives. Many are discovered only after adverse circumstances have forced a detour or set up seemingly impenetrable roadblocks to the pursuit of our original ambitions and goals.

That little observation quite neatly washed the starch right out of any excuse I might have harbored about there not being anything I could do even though I was lying flat on my back and had only partial use of one arm and hand. But it didn't do a thing toward solving the problem of just which of my (supposedly many) talents the Lord wanted me to develop. One thing was certain, if I did have talents they were surely latent at that point in my life.

As I lay in my bed one day, I angled my looking glass toward the east window just in time to see my two young cousins, Louann Walker, age seven, and Darlene Mitchell, age three, cross the highway in front of my grandparents' house and head my way. As I watched them coming down the hill with two puppies they were bringing to show me, I was reminded of the dozens of times my brother Bob and I had run away to our grandparents' house when we were children.

I am told I developed the habit of running away almost as soon as I could walk, and Bob, who was two years younger, joined me at an early age. Actually, making our getaway wasn't too difficult. However, things weren't exactly pleasant when our parents discovered our absence. The thought of Grandma Jones' cookies and other goodies made the excitement of running away to grandma's house more than worth what we knew we'd encounter later on.

There were many interesting things I was observing through that looking glass. I recalled so well the day-long lecture Dr. Willie Sutton, a well-known speaker in the educational field, gave to our senior graduating class. For an entire day the soft-spoken, snowy-haired gentleman sat on a folding chair on the stage of the auditorium and, alternating between a serious and a light vein, imparted advice and a philosophy of life culled from the wisdom and experience of his advanced years.

Over and over again that day Dr. Sutton returned to one phrase: "Open your eyes!" he thundered, and again, softly pleading, "Open your eyes." We were urged to open our eyes to the realities and the opportunities of life before us. We were challenged to set our goals high and to embark upon a course that would bring about their realization. We were challenged to examine our convictions in the light of truth and to preserve those that passed the test with the courage of David going out to meet Goliath.

I doubt that Dr. Sutton is still living, but as I have often reflected on his inspiring words, I am struck each time by the immortality of his message.

I could no longer run up the road as a carefree child; but I could open my eyes, and through the aid of the looking glass, I could participate in life and living.

*As one whom his mother
comforteth, so will I comfort
you. (Isa. 66:13)*

## MY ANGEL MOTHER

Scientists have succeeded in developing instruments sensitive enough to measure the weight and thickness of particles so fine as to be visible only with the most powerful microscope. They have calculated the energy generated by hurricanes; estimated the distance of the stars; and sent rockets zooming toward the moon with amazing accuracy. But they have never discovered a way to measure the unselfish breadth, the sacrificial summit, the prayerful depths, or the comforting touch of a mother's love.

It was Abraham Lincoln who said, "All that I am, all that I hope to be, I owe to my angel mother." There are many who hold their mothers in the same high esteem as did Abe Lincoln, myself included.

It was my mother who realized my need for more than physical comfort if I was to find happiness on the tiny white island on which I suddenly found myself marooned. And it was she who understood my desire to accomplish something worthwhile.

In high school, my most cherished dream career-wise had been to be an English or home economics teacher even though I realized I could not go on to college. Still the dream persisted. Now it seemed that everything I attempted or considered dead-ended in "If only . . ."

For instance, if only I could sit up straight in a wheelchair. If only I could use a typewriter. If only I could hold a telephone receiver.

In the midst of my encounter with all these brick walls, I began to realize that even as God was closing certain doors, he was preparing to cut new ones that would swing open on ever more meaningful adventures and experiences. Eventually, we did find a way for me to operate the typewriter and the telephone.

While others were asking, "Why does Margaret Jean want to do this or that?" Mother was encouraging me to pursue my interest in writing. In high school I had won a couple of cash prizes in county-wide essay contests sponsored by the local chapter of the Veterans of Foreign Wars (VFW). I enjoyed creative writing, and from time to time after I became bedfast, I amused myself by writing short, humorous stories or essays based on my observations of what was going on around me. Most of these promptly found their way into the always overflowing wastebasket. A few were filed away.

Shortly after my return from NIH, my mother presented me with a couple of textbooks on fiction and feature writing. "Learn to write for publication," she encouraged.

"But what will I write about and, anyway, the manuscripts have to be typed," I countered.

"Well, go ahead and start writing. You can find plenty of subjects, and maybe a way will turn up to get them typed," she replied with a wisdom I failed to fully appreciate at the time.

I wasn't really all that confident of my abilities, but the idea did appeal to me. I began to tackle the challenge eagerly. Then one day a friend stopped by and, upon learning what I was trying to do, suggested that I might be able to use a small portable typewriter if it was placed on a low tray that just barely touched my stomach. It just so happened that he had one he wasn't using, and he brought it over the next day.

I found that I could reach all the keys with my right hand, but I could not reach the carriage return lever on the manual machine or sit straight enough to see the line of type to check for errors. Having taken typing lessons in high school, I was familiar with keyboard arrangement—which was good because I couldn't see the tops of the keys, only the front edge.

With a great deal of hard practice, I eventually solved the problem of not being able to see the line of words by learning to type with a fairly high degree of accuracy. When I knew that I had struck the wrong key, Mother would erase the letter, and I would correct the word before removing the page from the typewriter. I returned the carriage using a piece of heavy gauge wire cable with a hook on the end which had been devised by my father.

In the beginning, learning to type with one hand was hard work and slow going, but I had a goal to strive for and I stubbornly stuck with it. It was mother who helped me solve the mechanics of mastering the typewriter with only one hand, and it was she who set up the tray for me every day. It was she who filed my notes and patiently searched for the ones I needed. And it was Mother who obtained the books I wanted. She did these things all through the years until her own physical problems made it increasingly difficult and then impossible.

One day, someone asked why in the world I wanted to put myself and my mother to so much trouble when it would be much easier just to watch television. This attitude, I have learned, is unfortunately much too prevalent among normal people, and even more unfortunately, among many of the handicapped. To many people it comes as a distinct shock when I say that I have yet to watch my first television soap opera!

My mother was my writing assistant in addition to her duties as nurse, cook, maid, laundrywoman, seamstress, gardener, and wife of a busy farmer, just because she wanted me to have a full life. In my mother I have seen that the vastness of a mother's love has no room for despair. I have had much time and opportunity to analyze the indestructible qualities that constitute a mother's love. The boundaries of that love are illimitable. Daily I have thanked God that he saw fit to endow mothers with such infinite tenderness and that my mother saw fit to lavish it upon me.

Much annoyed by the "Why try?" attitude of people, I wrote something on the subject. It eventually became the basis for the first article I submitted to a magazine for consideration, in 1963. I was thrilled when *American Mercury Magazine* (no longer in existence) accepted my article. My elation was short-lived however. When the article appeared it was unrecognizable as my original work. The editor had salvaged my novel ideas and rewritten

them using such fancy language that I had no idea
what many of the words even meant. It was some
small consolation when a school teacher friend with
an M.A. degree confessed that he, too, was unfamiliar
with the words!

In my disappointment, I wondered if this was a
common practice among editors. I'm thankful to say I
have since learned it isn't. I was to learn, however,
that editors either reject something outright, accept
it as it is with minor revisions, or ask the author to
make any major revisions necessary.

Meanwhile, a very dear friend, seeking to encourage my writing career, presented me with a brand
new lightweight portable typewriter. Only three
inches high at the back, it was light enough so that I
could slide the end of the carriage around facing me
to reach the knob and insert the paper myself.

Still later, I acquired a more rugged model, and my
mother once again patiently inserted the pages for
me. The manual operation proved to be excellent
exercise for my finger and arm muscles. It wasn't
until after the publication of my first book on the
history of my native Cullman County, Alabama, in
1972, that I acquired an electric machine which took
all the labor out of typing (and a machine which for a
time, I discovered, had a mind all its own).

After Mother could no longer help me insert the
paper, I began to use computer paper cut in lengths of
three or four sheets which were cut apart after being
removed from the typewriter.

When I first began submitting articles for publication, my father announced grandly that he would
match dollar for dollar anything I earned. I'm not
sure whether his jest was prompted by his skepticism

of magazines really paying for articles or my ability
to write anything worth paying for.

"Be sure you hold him to that promise. We will be
your witnesses to back you up," laughed my Uncle
Hershel and Aunt Fanny who were visiting at the
time.

I had received no payment for the first article, but
early in 1963, I received a check for thirty-five dollars
from a religious magazine called *Youth's Instructor*.
The editor also asked if I would write another article
for him. Then came a check from the *Birmingham
News Monthly Magazine*.

Each time I received a check I triumphantly waved
it before Daddy and silently held out my hand. After
the third payoff he declared the deal void, but I still
get a kick out of reminding him of it.

In addition to magazine articles, I began writing a
weekly column for the local *Cullman Times* called
"Through the Looking Glass." The title of the
column, as you might guess, was inspired by events
and things around me, the people I met, and
sometimes my personal opinions, all making their
appearance in the small hand mirror I use to see what
is going on around me.

This fact alone provided the inspiration for several
amusing incidents which were written up and
appeared in the column. One such incident was the
time one of my doctors at NIH accused me of being the
vainest person he had ever met because he caught me
with a little mirror in my hand nearly every time he
entered my room. He was very skeptical of my
explanation that I had been using it to watch
activities down on the street seven stories below.
After putting his head close to mine on the pillow,

and angling the mirror in the position I showed him, he said, "I've got another patient who sits and counts her wrinkles all day. I'll have to tell her about your new game." Then he walked out of the room muttering that my discovery was worthy of being recorded.

Years later, when I was again hospitalized, a Catholic priest who visited all the patients each evening made the same accusation, as did also a head nurse at the nursing home. The nurse's remark was laughingly reported to me by an aide who had already discovered my real use of the mirror. But even the knowledge that my reputation for vanity was becoming widespread wasn't enough to inspire me to curtail my observations of my surroundings!

My relatives and friends had long since grown accustomed to my peering at them through the mirror which had become so much a part of me that it seldom occurred to me to wonder what kind of weird thoughts strangers might be having. Many of my readers were familiar with the allusion behind my choice of title and sometimes, on the rare occasions when I attended a public function, people would discover who I was and come over to ask where the mirror was. (It was always in my purse, but unless I was in my local community where everybody knew me, I seldom had the courage to bring it out.)

One day, the pastor of a nearby church, whom I had met through mutual friends, brought a visiting evangelist to see me. After the introductions were made and the preachers were taking seats across the room to my right, I casually picked up the mirror so that I could see them as we talked. No sooner had I done so than the evangelist exclaimed, "Oh, I know who you are now. You write that column for the paper, don't you?"

During the nine years I wrote the column for the *Cullman Times* I often awoke in the mornings wondering what surprises the day would bring. And there were many. By means of letters, telephone calls and interviews, and visitors who came knocking at our door (sometimes strangers accompanied by mutual friends, not infrequently people who introduced themselves by saying they read the column and wondered if they could come in for a minute to meet me), I became acquainted with scores of fascinating people from all walks of life and formed many beautiful friendships which are still enriching my life.

*This also I saw, that it was from the hand of God. (Eccles. 2:24)*

# WAXING ELOQUENT

A number of years ago, Art Linkletter asserted that kids say the darndest things, and he wrote a couple of very funny books to prove his point.

I happen to know some parents and grandparents who are inclined to agree. But no matter how many collections are made of such sayings, there is no chance of plagiarism because no two youngsters are apt to make the same observation or reach the same conclusion.

The funny sayings of children have provided me with some of my choicest ideas for "Through the Looking Glass" columns. Unfortunately, the strangeness of my situation, coupled with the fact that my hospital bed is too high for many children, has a tendency to inhibit the conversation of some of my young friends, especially if it happens to be a first visit. However, a simple explanation in response to their query, "Why are you like that?" usually serves to put them at ease.

One young man, however, who at the age of four had conquered all signs of shyness, was quite confident he had the answer to my confinement. But after walking all around my bed a couple of times and inspecting it carefully, he looked up at me quizzically.

"Where is your baby?" he asked.

It seems he had recently visited several homes every one of which had a new baby whose mother had just come home from the hospital.

Friends and relatives formed the habit of sharing their young friends or children's observations about life and living with me. These second-hand accounts gave me many laughs.

Everyone in our family was sure the Lord gave Darlene, then age three, credit for her table grace even though she confused matters a bit when she bowed her head and solemnly intoned, "Thank you, Hotdog, for Jesus."

This was the same young lady who, upon seeing her uncle kiss his wife of more than fifteen years, remarked knowingly, "If you two keep that up you will have to get married."

And it was also Darlene who on being confronted with a command from her father backed up by a stern "Did you hear me?" brightly replied, "No I'm not wearing my hearing aid today."

But it was six-year-old Bob who posed the sixty-four dollar question that intrigued his father and left his mother speechless.

"Mother," he said, "Daddy said we are going to see Papa Jones tomorrow. Are we?"

"If Daddy says so. He's the boss," his mother replied.

"He is?" Bob asked incredulously. "Then how come you are always saying, 'Tal, do this, and Tal, do that, and Tal, DON'T do that?' "

Not only children, but the changing seasons moved
the writer in me to wax eloquent. Tucked away in a
box, I found columns long since forgotten, but as I
worked on this book, these came to view.

Whoever named the month of March named it well. For
it is indeed the month when all things are on the move
from the first stirrings of nature awakening from
winter's slumber, to little boys with baseball bats in
hand, to farm tractors chewing up the moist earth, to
applique quilts flapping on the clothesline.

But one doesn't really need a calendar to know that
Spring is about to come marching in. To herald its
arrival, the daffodils have begun waving their golden
trumpets almost by the time their little green leaves
have pushed their way high enough to be seen above the
last of the autumn leaves to signal the imminent
serenade of flowers.

Even February relented near the end of her short
reign and relinquished her last wintry grip to stage a
preview of Spring's pageant with balmy sun-kissed days
swept along on capricious breeze. Already, I have
spotted a pair of bluebirds, robins and sparrows
inspecting my favorite oak tree and the row of
apartments beneath it. But whatever interest they may
have had was hastily ditched when the five cats which
have taken up residence, set up a relay stakeout,
completely ignoring the blackbirds pecking and preen-
ing nearby like a flock of bantam chickens.

The little red-suited man busily "pumping" the
windmill on the fence post has long since conceded
defeat and hangs his arms tiredly while the wind powers
the yellow propellers with effortless impertinence.
Down the hill, newborn calves frolic in carefree
abandonment, competing with the little windmill for
sheer bursts of energy.

Stormclouds and raindrops jostle for their own
position in March's spectacular march into Spring,
sometimes setting the pace with the soft beat of

sparkling droplets pattering on the windowpane. Other times, crashing thunder and flashing lightning set a faster tempo that command full attention.

Observing this renewal of nature our hearts take on a renewal also. Impossible dreams seem a little less so. Hope that has lost some of its inspiration pulsates with new courage and determination. Goals that somehow fell short or failed are viewed and reviewed with fresh imagination. Old ideas are resurrected with new insights. New ideas are christened with enthusiasm.

And, despite any adverse circumstances, trials and frustrations, our hearts sing for the pure joy of being a part of God's great universe, sending our spirits soaring to new heights and our faith to greater depths.

This column gives you some idea of the world beyond my bedroom window—the world of the giant oak tree, the expanding vista of fields, the old homestead of my grandparents up the slight hill, the blue jays dive-bombing for worms in the garden, and the changing sky and cloud formations. The handiwork of God knows no boundaries. Indiscriminately, he has wielded his paintbrush with infinite skill, and the changing seasons have brought breathtaking beauty for me to enjoy. And always, I am moved beyond the world of nature itself, to ponder thoughts of the Almighty who is nature's Creator.

Even as this book is being written, springtime is just around the corner. And just as the world of nature experiences the miracle of renewal through God's loving touch, so should each person seek the inner renewal of his own soul. Take hope that just as God's world awakens to a new life of joyousness and the melodic strains of springtime, so can we redefine lofty ambitions and rededicate ourselves to the pursuit of those greater achievements and goals which may have been submerged by the gloom of a harsher season.

How appropriate that in the midst of this resurrection of the earth which makes one glad to be alive, comes the celebration of a greater Resurrection which brings the hope of eternal life. In the contemplation of this marvelous Master Plan, so filled with hope and encouragement, comes a deep sense of humility.

Humility that comes with the knowledge that man, for all his conquests, gadgets, and inventions, cannot create life—only help to nourish it. Man, for all his sophistication, cannot survive without the marvel of recreation with which the lowly seed has been endowed by an all-wise Creator.

Springtime, then, is the reminder anew that the world is, undisputably, God's universe, teeming with beauty and harmony and ours to enjoy simply for the price of a moment's humble pause.

What greater time than springtime to follow the example of King David by lifting one's gaze to the fertile hills to be reminded anew of the Source of one's help.

*For I have learned to find*
*resources in myself*
*whatever my circumstances.*
*(Phil. 4:11 NEB)*

# RESOURCES AND
# RESOURCEFULNESS

The little mirror became an inseparable part of me; it was my link to the world. At NIH I used it to look down on the street, to watch the falling snow, and later the lovely dogwood blossoms, the beautiful sunrises, and the lights of the city. At home I have used it for years to see the cotton fields and watch the people working in them. Angled rightly, I can see the pasture, pond, and cattle on the other side of the house. Someone asked me how I ever thought of using a mirror for the purpose of watching people. The truth is I really don't remember. I suppose it must have been just a spontaneous action born out of my frustration at not being able to turn my head to see on either side of the room or out the window.

If you look around, it is not hard to find any number of things being used for purposes other than their original one. For instance, bean pots become flower containers, doors serve as coffee tables, and farmers have even been known to use an electric blanket to keep a new litter of pigs from freezing! I've even heard of enterprising souls who use automobile radiators as moonshine distilleries!

With such ingenuity a commonplace thing, you wouldn't expect people to be so surprised to learn that a plain little old mirror from the dime store could be used for more things than keeping track of the aging lines in one's face.

Of course, my silvery companion dutifully serves its original purpose and keeps me well-informed on advancing age, but without exception I have found its other reflections more fascinating and more entertaining. In the course of catching all those reflections I have broken enough looking glasses to invite a lifetime of bad luck. Since I have not experienced any unusual amount, I gladly and thankfully offer my experience as conclusive proof that this old belief is completely unfounded.

Rear Admiral Richard E. Byrd, a devout Christian who believed strongly in the power of prayer, once wrote: "Few men during their lifetime come anywhere near exhausting the resources dwelling within them. There are deep wells of strength that are never used."

Many people have said to me, "I could never have your patience," or "I could never smile all the time like you do."

"Well, why not? You can if you want to, and if you have to," I counter.

Nobody ever knows what they can do until they try. The sad part is that all too often we never even take that all-important first step because we don't think we can do it. We forget, or perhaps have never learned, that the only real failure is the abandonment of hope and a will to try.

The monster called myositis ossificans progressiva forced me to find different ways of doing things at a very early age. I learned early that there are lots more ways of doing just about anything. I learned even sooner that especially when you are young it is just as well to experiment when there is no adult around to caution you about hurting yourself—or worse—to inform you that it simply can't be done that way.

Fortunately, when I was very young and the disease had first struck, I often had the house all to myself while everybody else was either hoeing or picking cotton. I took advantage of the situation to do all sorts of things, figuring that what nobody knew wouldn't hurt them.

I tackled the sewing machine and learned that I could operate one nicely by standing up to peddle the treadle and later—with the newer models—to press the toe button on an electric machine. Learning to sew straight was not quite so simple.

Then there was the matter of baking which I loved to do because Daddy had a sweet tooth and never failed to praise my efforts, however awful.

Most of the time Mother would set the ingredients I would need on the cabinet before she went to the field. But on those frequent occasions when a sudden impulse struck in the middle of a dull afternoon, a chair pulled up to the cabinet and climbed on to reach upper shelves sufficed nicely. A knife handle made a great extension for my limited arm reach in tapping the knob to turn on the oven. The oven rack could also be pulled out when my goodies were done, and the knife prevented my getting burned.

Even today, I still read books on how to do things I

can't possibly do. Sometimes, I generously share my
"expert" knowledge with someone who is about to
undertake a project. I usually get the same skeptical
response to my helpfulness. "What do you know
about that? You've never tried it."

"Well, that's what the book said."

"Books don't know everything. Anyway there is a
lot of difference in telling somebody how to do
something and doing it."

"Maybe," I reply, "but I learned how to crochet
pretty good one time by reading a book."

End of argument. But still my advice isn't always
trusted.

One night my telephone rang, and a man, whom I
had first met some months earlier when he came by
selling insurance, asked me to come and speak to his
young-adult Sunday school class. I was stunned
speechless. *I*, who had a horrible dread of oral reports
in school and avoided them whenever possible and
who now felt self-conscious among strangers, was
being asked to speak to a group of total strangers. It
was absolutely unthinkable.

I began making excuses. It had been fifteen years
since I'd stood before a group, and that occasion was a
stammering and stuttering disaster. Memories of
those classroom ordeals came flooding back as I tried
to convince Mr. Turner that the whole idea was
impossible and ridiculous.

Trying a new tactic, I explained how difficult it
was for me to be put into a car. Because my body is
rigid, I have to sit out on the edge of the seat and
lean against the back, sort of like a telephone pole.
My auto trips were rare and far between, and
mostly, at that time in my life, short excursions

with maybe a stop in a friend's driveway for a brief chat.

This fine Christian gentleman wasn't going to let me off the hook. He told me that he'd been inspired to ask me because of his concern for a young couple who had recently experienced a great tragedy. They were groping to regain their faith. Perhaps my experience might be an inspiration to them as well as to the rest of the class. He neatly dispensed with my last excuse by offering to drive the fifteen miles from his home to help get me into the car.

Even as I made each excuse, I couldn't get away from the knowledge that as followers of Christ we are bidden to witness for him. "Pray about it, Margaret, and call me back. I'm sure you will do as God leads," Mr. Turner told me.

Unable to sleep, I wrestled with this impossible request. "Lord, you know I don't have any talent as a speaker. Anyway, I don't know what to say. I'll just make an idiot out of myself," I prayed anxiously.

"That's right, you will. You know you can't do it," the devil whispered.

Then, seemingly out of nowhere, came a reminder of God's message to Paul after the apostle had pleaded for the removal of his own affliction which he felt impeded his effectiveness as a tool for spreading the gospel of Christ: "My grace is sufficient for you, for my power is made perfect in weakness" (II Cor. 12:9 RSV).

"Okay, Lord, I'll speak to that class, but how big a disaster it is depends on you because you know better than I do what a lousy speaker I am," I prayed with little faith and trepidation. Not until later did I see the incongruity of my worry in the face of God's promise of strength for every need and the proof of it in my life already. I wasn't granted an instant gift of oratory, but God proved once again that he does provide for our needs if the spirit is willing to do his bidding.

I think my reticence at being among strangers disappeared that day in the Sunday school class. After that, I thoroughly enjoyed chatting freely with strangers who would stop by my chair to speak to me wherever I went. I was never again bothered by people staring at me or my unusual chair.

I am still much more comfortable behind a typewriter than I ever was in front of a microphone, but I now know the Lord can do wonders with butterflies in one's stomach!

In his letter to the Corinthian Christians, the apostle Paul wrote: "Now therefore perform the doing of it; that as there was a readiness to will, so there may be a performance also out of that which ye have. For if there be first a willing mind, it is accepted according to that a man hath, and not according to that he hath not" (II Cor. 8:11-12).

Clearly then, God is telling us not to waste physical, mental, and spiritual resources that he has entrusted to us. Whether they be many or few, humble or great, he appoints to us the responsibility of making the best possible use of them for his glory. And you can count on it, he does bless those efforts. It is the Creator's prerogative to endow some with seemingly limitless opportunities, while placing hard restrictions on others.

Jesus taught a lesson to Peter, albeit in a different context, but the meaning is applicable when we are tempted to question the Almighty's judgment. Peter questioned Jesus about John (another of Jesus' disciples). Very bluntly, Jesus replied, "What concern is it of yours. You follow me!" (John 21:22 TAB).

The apostle Paul assures us that so long as we are willing to submit to God's will for our lives, he looks upon honest effort that may have ended in failure and sacrifices that may not have seemed much to others with as much favor as the greater works accomplished by those who are more ably endowed. In Jesus' eyes, the widow's mite was just as significant as more lavish gifts.

We cannot give more than we have, but we can give all we have to whatever task is at hand, confident that sufficient strength will be there. God created each of us unique, "Designer Originals," giving us the weaknesses and strengths that shape the pattern of the life he has chosen for us to follow.

Just as an automobile must tax its engine to the utmost in an effort to negotiate an icy hill or treacherous mountain incline, so are our own inner resources—and, yes, our faith—often stretched beyond what seems to be the breaking point in the face of hardships, tragedies, trials, and sorrows.

*If I must boast, I will boast
of the things that show my
weakness. (II Cor. 11:30 RSV)*

# REHABILITATION FROM WITHIN

Disability, like intelligence, is more a matter of degree than of kind. It is more a question of attitude than of aptitude.

Webster defines a handicap as "a disadvantage that makes achievement usually difficult." Difficult, perhaps, in the face of unconventional or compensatory methods and a barrage of obstacles ranging from physical to social to environmental assumptions—but certainly not impossible.

And achievement may not always come in one's originally preferred field—but not infrequently in something which one comes to find even more rewarding. Since psychologists have said that everyone has more than a thousand latent talents of which one is often unaware, one's potential is limited only by one's determination to succeed, if not in one's chosen field then in something equally fulfilling.

If one has the will to be rehabilitated from within, then the means is only a matter of opportunity. According to that premise, new talent can and must be nourished and allowed to bear fruit.

Opportunity rarely comes as an unbidden visitor to anyone's door, and for the handicapped it is an even rarer event. The disabled are forced to exercise even greater diligence in the search of it; but, unfortunately, a survey showed that nearly 60 percent of those interviewed had no idea where to turn for needed aid and guidance in seeking to overcome handicaps.

One of the biggest stumbling blocks is none other than Uncle Sam who, theoretically, is dedicated to helping the handicapped remove some of the boulders in their way. This is no little cause for frustration and despair among those who seek to overcome the disadvantages of physical and mental handicaps.

I learned of a severely disabled young man confined to a wheelchair who had earned a college degree but was unable to find employment in the field in which he qualified because of his handicap.

In a determined effort to become self-supporting, he established a small business. Although the income was not great, he worked hard to make his business a success, and he was very proud to be earning an income. His happiness was short-lived, however, when he learned that his small pension check would be stopped if he earned more than forty dollars per month. Both the pension and his earnings were barely enough to make ends meet.

Complicating this young man's dilemma, and that of many thousands of other handicapped people, is the fact that the loss of either Supplemental Security Income or Social Security Disability also means the loss of Medicaid and Medicare coverage. Few handicapped people can afford the very high premiums of private medical insurance in those few cases where it can be obtained. For many, the price of personal dignity is literally too high.

Many handicapped people are not physically capable of full-time jobs outside their homes. Others are unable to find employment in the regular work force. But through sheer willpower, determination, and perseverance, many have made heroic efforts to earn some income through home-based businesses or hobbies only to be told by the powers that be that if they desire to do their own thing, then their pensions will be stopped.

It is a vicious circle. On the one hand, millions of dollars are being spent on the successful rehabilitation of the severely disabled while at the same time much human potential—the greatest of all natural resources—is being destroyed by governmental regulations that in effect encourage the handicapped to sit and watch the world go by rather than become contributors to society.

According to HEW statistics, five hundred thousand people become disabled each year through injury and disease. The Vietnam War resulted in the permanent maiming of more than 250,000 people. The human suffering is incalculable.

But equally immeasurable is the raw courage and grit of these unfortunate people as they struggle to pick up the pieces of shattered lives. Immeasurable, too, are the feelings of renewed hope and self-esteem that come with the accomplishment of being able to do something constructive.

A physical or mental handicap frequently necessitates a detour. It need not and should not mean the end of the road. There are always alternative routes that, although sometimes rough and rocky, can lead to fulfillment if incentive is not destroyed.

If life is to have meaning it must have a purpose and goals. And the motivation behind that purpose is a desire for personal achievement and dignity, to accept challenge, to enjoy the opportunity of developing one's abilities, whether large or small, to the fullest extent possible.

To destroy the incentive for self-betterment through the withdrawal of vital financial support is a tragic waste of creativity and initiative. The high cost of rehabilitation and the much higher cost of personal perseverance is futile if governmental regulations stifle the development of that potential.

The time is long overdue for a new look at penalizing rules. The fact that a handicapped person's basic cost of living is usually higher than average because of frequent medical and drug bills, the high cost and upkeep of prosthetic devices, special equipment, clothing and/or diets, and attendant care must be taken into consideration. At the present time most pensions will not adequately cover these costs.

Present regulations need to be changed to allow the severely disabled to earn a realistic amount before the pension is reduced or discontinued and to allow a higher level of personal earnings before Medicaid or Medicare coverage is lost.

Not only is economic welfare at stake, but the equally important restoration of self-esteem. Rehabilitation from within is of far greater import than any other consideration.

*Rejoicing in hope; patient
in tribulation; continuing
instant in prayer.
(Rom. 12:12)*

# VICTIM OR VICTOR?

The April 1977 issue of *Reader's Digest* told the story of David Hartman of Havertown, Pennsylvania, who was determined to become a medical doctor despite the fact that he had been totally blind since the age of eight. Upon his enrollment at Gettysburg College, his faculty advisor tried to steer him toward other fields, but David had his heart set upon becoming a psychiatrist.

Following his graduation from college with a 3.8 average out of a possible 4.0, he applied for admission to ten medical schools. Nine of the schools immediately rejected his application, but Dr. M. Prince Brigham, assistant dean of admissions and student affairs at Temple University School of Medicine in Philadelphia, convinced his fellow admission board members that in the face of what David had already proved, they should fling their doors open to him.

Medical courses, tough and challenging for seeing students, became even more so for David. He was faced with learning anatomy and histology by feeling the formaldehyde-preserved cadaver with his hands and listening to descriptions by his classmates and teachers. But he made it! Upon receiving his M.D. degree in 1976, Dr. David Hartman immediately began a six-year rotating residency that will further qualify him as a psychiatrist and specialist in rehabilitative medicine.

"I'm really no different from anyone else because everybody has some kind of disability. I believe the ones who are most handicapped are those who don't want to do anything special or challenging with their lives," Dr. Hartman said of his determination to fulfill an impossible dream.

In the Bible, the apostle Paul set a marvelous example of triumphing over trials and adversities of every magnitude, ranging from physical afflictions to personal dangers, as he traveled to spread the gospel of Christ. He could say,

> We are handicapped on all sides, but we are never frustrated; we are puzzled, but never in despair. We are persecuted, but we never have to stand it alone: we may be knocked down but we are never knocked out! Every day we experience something of the death of Jesus, so that we may also know the power of the life of Jesus in these bodies of ours . . . . We wish you could see how all this is working out for your benefit, and how the more grace God gives, the more thanksgiving will redound to his glory. This is the reason that we never collapse. The outward man does indeed suffer wear and tear, but every day the inward man receives fresh strength. These little troubles, which are really so transitory, are winning for us a permanent, glorious and solid reward out of all proportion to our pain. (II Cor. 4:8-10, 15-17 based on Phillips)

Like an engine or product that must be put through many stresses and endurance tests before it is perfected, we, too, must be willing to undergo trials and challenges, sometimes to the limits of *our* endurance, if we want our own faith to grow.

In industry it sometimes takes a tragic accident, like the crash of the DC-10 airplane some years ago which was attributed to the faulty design of the door and resulted in the loss of many lives, to force attention to a weakness and bring about the necessary changes to make the construction stronger. God also uses our weaknesses and failures to make us stronger and more capable of negotiating life's stormy seas. When things are going smoothly we really don't have much incentive to test the fabric of our inner resources. But adversity, if it is to be overcome, requires strong fabric. How blessed that God's plans always include the strength to repair the rent or to redesign our lives through a deeper utilization of the inner resources which are God's unique gift to us. We can become victims or victors.

Any ordeal can be met and coped with more patiently when one comes to the realization that the strenuous and painful testing of our faith through hardships and difficulties can be the means of developing greater strengths. In times of hardship "latent" resources will surface and with them a firmer faith, renewed hope, and determined resolve.

Shortly after I began writing for publication, the editor of *Youth's Instructor* sent me a back issue of the magazine containing an article about one of his long-time poetry contributors and suggested that I might enjoy getting acquainted with her. Touched by the lovely poems in the several magazines which the editor had thoughtfully included, I wrote the author a short note telling her how much I admired her poetry for its beautiful expression of thought.

Promptly, a warm and friendly reply came back, and thus began a prolific and inspiring correspondence with one of the most remarkable persons I have ever known.

By the time I came to know Jane Merchant of Knoxville, Tennessee in 1963, she had already been confined to bed for more than thirty-one years. Born with osteogenis imperfecta, a brittle bone disease for which there is no known cure, Jane had suffered so many fractures by the age of twelve that she was no longer able to sit in a wheelchair. Always hard of hearing, she had become totally deaf at the age of twenty-three. She was also nearly blind and forced to use hot compresses daily in an effort to conserve her remaining sight.

She was the author of more than three hundred poems published in various magazines and five books of poetry. Her first volume, *The Greatest of These*, had been awarded first prize by the National League of American Pen Women for the best work of poetry by a League member. She later wrote five more books, incuding some delightful volumes of light verse.

Believing devoutly that if one can't make light of his troubles they are best kept in the dark, Jane seldom mentioned her problems in her letters except to make some humorous comment about something that had gone awry and always to look optimistically on the brighter side of any situation. Her letters sparkled with the keen wit, refreshing thoughts, and

quiet but deeply abiding faith in God that was
reflected in her poems.

In one of her boks, *Think About These Things,* Jane
bares the agony of a soul fired with desire and
tortured by helplessness as she pleads humbly:

> What shall I do, O Father, with
>     this sadness?
> Is there a use that I can put it to . . .
> Let this sadness not be wasted in self-pity
> Let it be somehow, O Lord, of service unto thee.

Unable to attend school at all, Jane was taught to
read and write by her two older sisters, her brother,
and her mother. Each day she eagerly awaited the
school lessons of her sisters and brother who always
shared what they had learned that day with her.

She loved books but was forced to curtail her
exploration of them to conserve her eyesight.
Refusing to indulge in self-pity, she began to express
her innermost thoughts, reflections, and observations in poetry. Blessed with deep insights that led
her to find inspiration in everything from a tiny
spider on her windowsill and the brief expanse of the
outside world observed from her bedroom window, to
the conflicts and victories waged within her own
breast, she turned her sadness into a challenge that
enabled her to serve God and bring joy to her
fellowman in a most rewarding way.

In another one of her books entitled *The Mercies of
God* she writes:

> Grant us to give the smallest
>     task our best. . . .

Yet not shirk from the
largest task through fear.

Even after a radical mastectomy—necessitated by malignancy—greatly curtailed the use of her arm, Jane continued to write and publish other books. Many of her readers never knew about the afflictions that were a lifelong companion of this courageous lady with a singing heart.

Characteristic of my beloved friend's valiant spirit and her desire to spare those around her from her pain, the first intimation I had that all was not well came in a brief note tucked in a Christmas card. "At the moment my typewriter is gathering dust in the corner, but maybe it won't always be so," she wrote and then went on to tell how her family planned to spend Christmas. Three weeks later, she died at the age of fifty-one, a radiant witness to the power of faith to raise one above the clutches of adversity.

Four walls imprisoned Jane Merchant's frail body for more than forty years, but they were not strong enough to confine her free spirit and genuine enjoyment of life which was made even richer by her love for all people. Instead of withdrawing from the world, she observed it with rare perception and understanding. Then through the clarity of profound thought and freshness of expression she gently and effectively injected into a society all too often driven by a hectic pace and preoccupation a sense of joy and renewed hope, a keener awareness of the beauty and pleasure in even the most ordinary things, and a humble sense of gratitude for all things.

In her willing struggle to put forth her best efforts to make the most of life, she succeeded in bringing the world to her own doorstep and breaking down her prison walls.

In the words of the apostle Paul, people like Jane Merchant have put their resources to the test and found them adequate: "Rejoicing in hope; patient in tribulation; continuing instant in prayer" (Rom. 12:12).

Through the example of her and of others, I have come to the place where I can say—even as Paul did—"I have learned, in whatsoever state I am, therewith to be content" (Phil. 4:11).

*Whatsoever thy hand findeth
to do, do it with thy might.
(Eccles. 9:10)*

# MONUMENT OR
STUMBLING BLOCK?

In the preface of *Man or Superman,* the famous
author, George Bernard Shaw, wrote:

> This is the true joy in life, the being used for a mighty
> purpose, recognized by yourself as a mighty one. The
> being thoroughly worn out before you are thrown on
> the scrap heap, the being a force of Nature instead of a
> selfish clod of ailments and grievances, complaining
> that the world will not devote itself to making you
> happy.

For years, the familiar and reassuring old hymn,
"Nearer My God to Thee," has been one of my
favorites. It was after reading the story of the sinking
of the *Titanic,* in which the band began playing this
hymn as the doomed passengers aboard ship went to
a watery grave, that I first began to appreciate the
depth of its so beautifully expressed message. I often
played Tennessee Ernie Ford's inspiring recording of
the hymn, and my heart was always warmed by its
comforting words. Then one day I came across the

touching story of how Sarah Flower Adams came to
write this grand old hymn, and I appreciated the
words even more.

From childhood, Miss Adams had wanted to
become a great stage actress. She devoted long hours
of study and hard work to the accomplishment of her
goal. Eventually, she was given a lead role in a
Shakespeare play and became a widely acclaimed
star. But her happiness turned to bitter heartbreak a
short time later when she was overtaken by a serious
illness which left her weakened and permanently
incapacitated.

A devout Christian, she turned to her Bible for
comfort and courage. Gradually, she began to express
her innermost thoughts and emotions in verses
which were published in various magazines. Three
years after the onset of her illness, her pastor
persuaded her to contribute some hymns for a
hymnbook he was compiling.

One day weeks later, the pastor stopped by to get
the hymns and found her in a state of depression. She
confessed that she had not been in the mood to write
and began to complain about the unfair circumstances which had deprived her of going on with her
cherished life goal. Quietly, the minister turned her
thoughts to the story of Jacob's vision at Bethel in the
Old Testament and suggested that she read it.

She turned to Genesis 28 and once again read of
Jacob's mission to Padan-aram to get a wife. Enroute
he stopped for a night's rest. His sleep was disturbed
by a dream in which a ladder extended from earth to
heaven with angels descending and ascending. The
Lord stood above it and spoke to Jacob. When he
awoke he knew that the Lord had been there, and he

vowed a vow. Then he took a stone and erected it as a pillar and called the name of the place "Bethel."

It wasn't the first time her pastor had suggested she read that passage. But this time as she read it she saw the connection between the story and her own life with its illness and disappointments. Inspired by this insight, she took up her pen and wrote the hope-filled verses of "Nearer, My God, to Thee" almost without effort.

With a submissive will and a heart filled with praise and understanding of her own experience, she wrote:

> There let the way appear,
>   Steps unto heaven;
> All that thou sendest me,
>   In mercy given;
> Angels to beckon me
> Nearer, my God, to thee . . .
>   Nearer to thee!
>
> Then, with my waking thoughts
>   Bright with thy praise,
> Out of my stony griefs
>   Bethel I'll raise;
> So by my woes to be
> Nearer, my God, to thee . . .
>   Nearer to thee!

Because Miss Adams saw her own thwarted dreams as the "cross that raiseth me," and her illness, pain, and loneliness as steps unto heaven and turned them into a mighty force for good, countless people have been inspired to find renewed strength and comfort in the fresh realization and declaration that our woes can indeed draw us nearer to God.

In one way or another, each of us comes to our own Bethel when we are forced to wrestle with stony griefs and fears, problems and failures. The hardness of the pillow is often beyond our power to cushion with softer material to soothe the hurts and bruises and discomforts. But, like Jacob, we can make it a monument rather than a stumbling block, pouring over it the oil of determination and vowing with God's help to brighten our own little corner of the world with the best possible use of the resources at hand.

Most often, what looks like a dead-end street turns out, upon closer examination, to be only a sharp curve. Sometimes it is necessary to back up a bit and make a new approach before we can negotiate it, but when we become aware that God has planned the route and all the stops along the way, the adventure becomes one of joyous anticipation.

I am reminded, too, of Fanny Crosby who became blind at the age of six when a doctor maltreated an eye inflammation. She allowed herself to become a marvelous instrument for the communication of God's blessings after rising from her own physical fetters. She enrolled in the New York Institute for the Blind at the age of fifteen and then became a teacher there. She had a gift for verse and eventually some of her works were published and set to music.

Following her marriage in 1858 to Alexander Van Alstyne, a blind music teacher and church organist who had been one of her students, Miss Crosby devoted most of her time to writing hymns. By the time of her death in 1915 at the age of ninety-five, many of them had been published and widely circulated here and abroad.

How impoverished the world would be today were

it not for the beloved hymns of Fanny Crosby.
Perhaps one of the best known is "Safe in the Arms of
Jesus" which she composed in fifteen minutes. I
counted eleven of her hymns in one edition of the
*Cokesbury Worship Hymnal,* including such familiar
old favorites as "Blessed Assurance," "I Am Thine, O
Lord," "Praise Him," "Jesus Is Calling," and "Rescue
the Perishing." In "Close to Thee" Miss Crosby
writes:

> Not for ease or worldly pleasure,
> Nor for fame my prayer shall be;
> Gladly will I toil and suffer,
> Only let me walk with thee.

"To enjoy your work and to accept your lot in
life—that is indeed a gift from God. The person who
does that will not need to look back with sorrow on his
past, for God gives him joy" (Eccles. 5:19-20 TLB),
writes the Preacher in the book of Ecclesiastes.

Through a series of God-given coincidences, my
own hand had been guided toward creative writing
and I tackled it with might. Originally, it had been
pursued as a studied attempt for self-preservation
and a welcome weapon to fight boredom. But once the
"ink got to my veins," what started out as a mere
battle for survival became a victory over a shackled
body and spirit.

The gift spoken of by the writer of Ecclesiastes had
been given me abundantly, for not only had I been
granted the joy of acceptance of circumstances and a
means of fulfillment, but also blessings I had never
dreamed of. Daily they accumulated—enriching,
encouraging, challenging—waiting to burst forth at
exactly the right moment.

# WHEN GOD OPENS DOORS

The English essayist, Charles Lamb, wrote: "Not many things in life, and I include all urban and all rural sounds, exceed in interest a knock at the door."
I agree with the gentleman wholeheartedly. Whether it be created by the gentle tap of knuckles against the door jamb or the insistent rap of a wooden knocker or the musical tinkle of a doorbell, the knock at the door commands instant attention. It produces a feeling of curiosity, anticipation, and apprehension all mixed up in an emotional jumble which can only be untangled when one acknowledges the sound by responding to it.

A knock at the door is the sound of promise. Behind it one may find delight or dismay, surprise or shock, pleasure or pain.

A knock at the door may mean the sound of friendship, thoughtfulness in action, news in actuality, excitement in depth, or fear in full dimension.

A knock at the door may signal the prelude of routine breaking, loneliness fleeing, horizon stretching, adventure calling, disaster looming. It can be the announcement of opportunity arriving, persistence pleading, resistance crumbling, and bills due!

At our house a knock at the door is always a welcome sound which creates an air of expectancy. People have come from all parts of the country and from all walks of life. They have brought with them a bit of the outside world and left behind the memory of a pleasant visit. He who can ignore a knock at the door has more resistance than I. He also misses an opportunity to enjoy an interesting or unusual experience.

Many of my new friends and the people I met through the newspaper column were retired senior citizens. Their accounts of local history fascinated me. The legends and folklore inspired both my interest and my curiosity. I was so intrigued by their tales of the past that, without realizing it, I became a local history buff.

I often made notes about some fact that I had not known before. Occasionally, I devoted one of my columns to a little-known historical fact or legend or way of life in the "good old days." Many times, these stories jogged someone else's memory and they would call or write me a letter. Thus my collection just sort of grew spontaneously. The South has always been of interest to historians particularly as it relates to the Civil War and the Reconstruction period. I was living in the very heart of this country and the material that came to my attention was nothing short of mind-boggling.

Then, in 1970, an item in the local paper noted that a committee was being appointed to formulate plans for the county centennial celebration three years away. The article mentioned that no history exclusively of Cullman County had ever been written. Many historical facts were fast becoming lost to posterity—or in some cases might already be lost.

"There's your opportunity. You write the history," mother suggested.

The idea was startling. Until that moment, I had never even thought of tackling a project of such magnitude. In the first place, I knew practically nothing about book publishing except that it was costly and that most authors of local history had to finance the book themselves. My knowledge of the county in which I had been born some thirty-five years before, and never left, was not much greater than my book publishing savvy. But I did know one thing for sure: based on my conversations with elderly friends, there was a historical richness in Cullman County, Alabama, well worth preserving if it could be ferreted out after all these years.

I knew it would take a tremendous amount of research through what data was available in old newspaper files and even more digging to verify the information and fill in the missing gaps. I had never even been to the extreme western section of the county where the earliest settlements had originated; nor, with the exception of one man, a retired school teacher whom I had met through my writing, did I personally know anyone living in that section nearly fifty miles from my home. I was quite familiar with the eastern section but how, I wondered, could I accurately write about the territory I had never seen.

But even before I had decided to investigate the possibility of going ahead with such a tremendous undertaking, and even before I had sought God's guidance and help, he was already opening doors for me.

A preliminary telephone call to Mrs. Marguerite Rigsby, the director of the local library and a dedicated history buff, brought enthusiastic encouragement. "Go ahead and write it. I'll do everything I can to help you," she urged.

Not only did this gracious lady make available every scrap of pertinent information in the library, including personally researched and xeroxed copies of valuable data in old books that were too heavy for me to handle, she also suggested people whom I might like to interview.

Next I mustered the courage to contact a prominent lawyer in the adjoining county who had written a three-volume history of the district he had once represented in the U.S. Congress and which included Cullman County. He kindly answered my questions about how his books were published and made what turned out to be an invaluable suggestion for the assurance of some financial help to defray publishing costs.

When I began the actual research I was in for another surprise. I discovered that half of the 250 churches in the county were Missionary Baptist. I figured that that must place at least one in every community, large or small (and probaby nearly every crossroads too). I hit upon the idea of obtaining manuals from two associations which kept a complete list of all the Missionary Baptist churches and their pastors. I then called and asked each pastor if he could suggest some elderly citizen in his church or surrounding community who might be able to give me some early history about that area.

This worked extremely well. Often, the first people I contacted were able to give me much information and almost always were able to suggest someone else who might be of further help. I conducted more than five hundred telephone interviews, the vast majority of which were with complete strangers. I always simply stated my name and told them I was researching a book on the history of Cullman County. Not unless they invited me to come visit them did I tell them I was confined to bed.

Most of the people I called seemed keenly interested in the project and remarked that they were glad someone was doing it. I couldn't help being amazed at the number who often added, "I do hope you will get it right. One time the newspaper printed a story and it was all wrong."

Many times people would ask if I was the one who wrote that "Looking Glass" column for the paper. Then they would invariably refer to a certain essay that meant something to them—often they would refer to a column that had been written weeks or months earlier. Some, upon learning that I was unable to leave my home, asked if they could come to visit me and bring old documents.

As word of my research spread, people whom I had never even contacted began calling to volunteer all kinds of information, much of which I had no previous knowledge of. One day the sheriff, whom I had met during previous campaigns for office, stopped by and spent a couple of hours shedding new light on one of the oldest settlements in the county. His ancestors had been among the early settlers, and the stories had passed from one generation to another.

Another day, another candidate for office whom I had never met spent an entire afternoon talking with me about his history collection. An avid archaeologist and history buff, he later loaned me a precious record book containing valuable information on the founding and on the charter members of the oldest church in the county dating back to 1833.

The biggest and most humbling surprise of all came upon the publication of my book, *Combing Cullman County,* in 1972. Our local bookstore had agreed to sell copies, and my librarian friend had volunteered to place it on sale in the library. I had, however, counted on the responsibility of marketing the majority of the books on my own. I had a long list of advance orders which Daddy delivered immediately. A couple of days later I began receiving calls from friends and strangers alike asking if they could have some copies to sell for me. Among these were the tax collection probate judge and the owner (and descendant of the founder) of the oldest department store in the city of Cullman.

The book bore my name as author, but what made the book possible was the phenomenal response of scores of people just when I needed them most. While I never received a specific directive from God to write a history of Cullman County, I am convinced beyond doubt that it was he who guided my efforts so that my path led to exactly the right people. God wants to make the most of us, but we have to be willing to give him the worst of us. I eagerly responded to the door that opened for me in 1970, and it was a truly gratifying learning experience.

The publication of my first book led to the opening of some completely new doors. One of the first was an invitation by the local Rescue Squad to be the guest speaker at the state convention which was to be held in Cullman. I later received an invitation to review the book at Baileyton Junior High where I had attended school for nine years. (This was after myositis ossificans had completely locked my jaws, making it physically harder to speak in addition to my notable lack of talent in public speaking.)

Then the editor of the *Cullman Times,* which had carried my "Through the Looking Glass" column for nine years, called to ask if I would do a series of historical articles for a special centennial supplement in honor of the county's birthday. One of the regular reporters did some research in early editions of the paper for new facts and color or leads which I followed up with hundreds of hours of further digging and clarifying. When I wrote up this material it came to about fifty full-length articles. The 48-page supplement, which included many old photographs submitted by subscribers to the paper, won the first-place award for the best supplement of the year at the state convention of the Alabama Press Association in 1973.

The following January, I did another dozen full-length articles for the *Cullman Tribune,* the county's oldest newspaper which was celebrating its 100th anniversary. These articles formed the nucleus of my second book, *Cullman County Across The Years,* published in 1975.

Just as I had suffered a serious attack of myositis ossificans during the writing of my first book, I repeated the feat by suffering a severe attack on my left arm during the writing of *Across the Years.*

This left my arm even more paralyzed and for a

time it was very difficult to hold a clipboard which I used to write first drafts. I finally solved the problem of the wide gap between my two hands by getting a longer clipboard and holding it endways. An elastic band helped to hold the paper. Again, concentrating on finishing the book took my mind off the pain.

Writing these two books provided me with uncountable hours of pleasure. I also felt greatly privileged to be entrusted with the responsibility that went into the research, enlisting the help of others, and the actual writing of the books. I was happy and content in the doing of it.

"There is no duty we so much underrate as the duty of being happy," Robert Louis Stevenson said many years ago.

What is happiness? I have often asked that question as I have become an observer of human nature from the vantage point of my situation. Is happiness the accumulation of wealth? Then why are there so many divorces in money-rich Hollywood? Why so many stories of those who have resorted to the drug scene in an effort to fill up their lives? And what would prompt a wealthy businessman to put a gun against his temple and pull the trigger in his plush Wall Street office if wealth was a guarantee of happiness.

What is happiness? Is it good health? Then how do you explain the radiant smile that was a permanent part of Helen Keller. Or the enthusiasm of Dr. Chester Swor, noted author and lecturer who traveled thousands of miles spreading cheer and encouragement in his wake despite a childhood illness that left him lame?

In the first instance, wealth could not solve the

inner conflicts of a troubled mind and in the second, poor health could not confine the inner spirit of courageous souls.

Happiness is a definite quality. It is not made of "maybe if I had that I would be happy," or "if this thing had not occurred, life would have more joy for me." Rather, happiness is the ability to seek out something fine in the misfortunes or calamities that have invaded our lives.

Happiness is not a certificate of guarantee handed out like a slip of paper attached to an appliance guaranteeing it for the life of the article. Happiness comes with the willingness to accept circumstances as a challenge and in meeting that challenge with the best that is in you always.

Some time ago, Dr. Norman N. Bradburn, a University of Chicago psychologist, conducted a research project supported by the NIH in which he sought to determine why some people are happier than others. He chose four midwestern towns. One was prosperous, two were depressed, and one was average. After a thorough study and analysis, his conclusion was: "It is the lack of joy rather than the presence of sorrow that makes the difference."

Happiness, I have come to believe, is a distinctive characteristic of certain individuals. I'm not so sure I agree with Webster's definition of "happy" and "happiness." Webster says that to be happy is "to be favored by circumstances; to be lucky or fortunate; having, showing, or causing a feeling of great pleasure, contentment, joy." If happiness were dependent on good fortune, then a large proportion of people would never know happiness. Happiness is, I sense, more a state of mind than a state of being.

Among other things, happiness for me came to be defined as being in a comfortable position, having enough ideas to keep me writing the entire day, and knowing thoughtful editors who encouraged me and forwarded remarks by kind readers. To someone else happiness might be taking the last bale of a bounteous cotton crop to the gin or seeing a big pile of freshly laundered clothes all ironed and folded and ready to be put away. I find happiness in seeing the sun streaming through my window, a big stack of favorite records on the stereo, and having favorite friends knock on the door.

I have heard individuals say that happiness is walking in the rain, watching a football game, and camping in a remote mountain area. And so it goes. What brings happiness to one does not necessarily draw the same response from another. The important thing is that you discover and nourish the little kernel within you that can spark the beginning of a rich experience. A diligent gardener will soon find himself reaping a harvest of full-blown happiness. Not because life is a bed of roses, but because the individual has disciplined his life in such a way that healthy thoughts have choked out the gloom and a spirited outlook overshadows the disappointments.

There are open doors all around us; the point is, we need to be alert and watchful for those opportunities where we can go through the doors and in so doing step across the threshhold into enriching and satisfying experiences that bring happiness to ourselves and others.

*We are more than conquerors*
*through him that loved us.*
*(Rom. 8:37)*

# A NEW DIMENSION

Conquering an Everest, strewn with boulders of pain and physical limitations, and laced with crevices created by lack of educational opportunities, has always been the challenge confronting the handicapped. It was, therefore, more than a challenge to me personally to be asked to join a small group seeking to find ways to help the handicapped in our area.

About the time I began working on my first book, I was invited by Bob Dyer, a local vocational rehabilation counselor, to help organize a vocational workshop for the handicapped. I had met Mr. Dyer some months previous to this when I interviewed him for my newspaper column. I had expressed the wish then that there could be a facility to employ the handicapped. "I have known from personal experience the ravages of boredom," I told him. He revealed that this had long been one of his goals also.

A group of ten people held an organizational meeting in our home. I knew only two of this group, all of whom became charter board members. Some were parents of severely handicapped adults, others were special education teachers. I was the only handicapped person involved.

At our first meeting, we discussed names for our eventual facility. I toyed with several acronyms that would reflect some of the goals we hoped to achieve. One of these was IDEAL Industries which stood for *I*ndependence, *D*ignity, *E*mployment, *A*chievement, and *L*uster—the acronym being the sum total of what we hoped the other five words would add to the lives of the people the center would eventually serve. This suggestion was unanimously adopted and the word "Inc." was added.

Mr. Dyer served as the first elected president, and later I also had the honor of serving in that post for two years. During this period we staged several successful fund-raising events which included road blocks, rummage sales, gospel concerts, and even a wrestling match featuring a local attorney and a state legislator who was a professional wrestler.

I was able to help arrange the concerts and it was a busy and exhilarating time for me—though sometimes hectic. We encountered such problems as, no key to the building where the concert was being held and a piano that sounded like a tin washtub. Nevertheless, near calamity was averted each time at the last minute and our audience was never aware of what had happened.

Early in 1975, our application for a federal grant was approved and our dream for a facility moved closer to reality. At one of the board meetings, in my absence, the group moved to name the new facility the Margaret Jean Jones Adult Activities Center.

This came as an overwhelming surprise—an honor of which I am humbly proud.

The official sign posted in front of the center also carries the words: "Sponsored by Ideal Industries, Inc." The center's main goal is to provide meaningful training for its students to help prepare them to live a more normal life. For some students this means living independently, for others, living with minimal supervision.

The curriculum is divided into four major areas: Health Care, Personal Development and Guidance, Use of Leisure Time, and Pre-Vocational training. Each of these major units is further divided into subunits. The center is able to handle forty-two students and is open year-round.

Qualifications for acceptance at the center were kept simple. A prospective student must be eighteen years old. There are no other age restrictions. Upon entering the center each student is observed and tested, and an individualized Habilitation Plan written tailored to that particular student's needs. Since the center opened in 1975, it has been used to full capacity with many students' names yet on a waiting list. All who have had the advantage of attending the center attest that it has added a new and happy dimension to their lives.

Years ago, a well-meaning lady said to my mother: "I would come to visit your daughter, but I can't stand to see her so helpless." The belief that a disability automatically closes the door to opportunity and a satisfying life is held mistakenly by many people— and viewed with sadness and alarm by me. Most of us who are handicapped do not want to be pitied.

I won't soon forget the anguish in a friend's eyes as

she related the stinging criticism she had received for enrolling her mentally retarded daughter in a special class because, wrongly assumed the critic, "It is obvious she won't ever learn anything."

Another young mother, whose small son had a slight speech impediment, told of how she personally called on the parents of children similarly afflicted in an effort to stimulate enough interest to justify the hiring of a special speech teacher in the school system. "Would you believe," my friend related, "that many of those parents, some with children whose speech was almost unintelligible, refused to admit their child had a problem? Others were convinced the child would outgrow the defect or that putting him in a special class would mark him for life."

Parental pride and an unwillingness to face the facts have kept many a handicapped child from the advantages to be gained by seeking the right kind of help. These attitudes of pity, hopelessness, and fear of stigma are left over from the days when the handicapped were kept behind closed doors, the heirs to a legacy of neglect as far as rehabilitation is concerned. How dreadfully regretable that was.

Through the years, I have been deeply committed to helping handicapped people in whatever way I possibly could. I know there is a new dimension that can come into our lives when we are doing something. Seeing our dream of a facility to help the handicapped in our area become a reality has been one of the great blessings that has come into my life in recent years.

# LIKE THE BREATH OF A ROSE

Fame is the scentless sunflower, with
   gaudy crown of gold,
But friendship is the breathing rose, with
   sweet in every fold.
Oliver Wendell Homes

Just as one lovely rose is more beautiful than a whole bouquet of sunflowers, so is one true friend more precious than vast fortunes and worldwide fame. How much happier is the man living in a tiny cottage surrounded by friendly neighbors than is the haughty millionaire living in a magnificently columned mansion perched high on a lonely hilltop.

Fame and fortune can keep you surrounded by people but they cannot prevent loneliness. They can provide great luxuries but they cannot manufacture happiness. They can buy feigned love but they cannot purchase consolation. They can bring laughter but they cannot wipe away tears. Only true friends are capable of being with us in times of need and of giving life meaning and beauty.

Friendship is a priceless possession, but it cannot be locked away in a safety vault and expected to keep for special occasions like a diamond necklace. If it is to retain its value and be kept free from tarnish, it must be used constantly through shared experiences of our everyday living.

Friendship has been likened to a mighty chain, the links being a smile, a laugh, a tear, a clasp of the hand, a word of cheer. But often we do not realize the length or strength of this chain until sickness or trouble strikes and offers of help pour in from all sides.

Friends are an inspiration. They lift us up and offer encouragement in times of trial, solace in times of sorrow, and joy in times of good fortune. They are sympathetic listeners to our confidences and respond to our dreams and ambitions with enthusiasm. They strive to see only the good in us and overlook our faults with an understanding and forgiving nature. We may lose contact with some of our friends down through the years, but they are never really forgotten and our lives are made richer for having known them.

We had the honor of entertaining such friends in our home six months before the end of 1975—a year that was to be full of surprises. As a result of these friends, in the months that followed I was able to face up to the necessity of major surgery and the knowledge that there was a high risk of complications with a strength and serenity I had never before exoperienced so profoundly.

Mrs. Lou Bevill, wife of U.S. Representative Tom Bevill (D. Ala.), is a gracious lady who lives her deep religious faith in all her daily activities and quietly shares her Christian witness in words and deeds wherever she goes. When Mrs. Bevill came to call, she brought with her one of her personal friends, Mrs. Mary O'Rear.

During the course of conversation with Mrs. O'Rear, whom I had never met before, she remarked that she, too, was interested in writing and was planning to do a magazine article and maybe a book. When I inquired about the subject, she quietly began telling me the soul-tingling story of how, about two years before, God had miraculously healed her of a critical heart condition after heart specialists had given her about six weeks to live.

Mrs. Bevill, who was sitting nearest to us, was the only other lady present who was aware of this remarkable story. As my other guests caught snatches of our conversation, they began to sense something special, and all other conversation abruptly ceased. All listened with awe as Mrs. O'Rear told of her brush with death, the X-rays showing her heart to be critically damaged, God's voice speaking to her, and the reaction of her doctor who ordered a second set of X-rays before he agreed with unconcealed puzzlement that her heart was perfectly whole and absolutely free of scars—as she had known it would be before she went for X-ray confirmation.

I had not known on that sweltering June morning that Mrs. O'Rear was going to be in the group visiting me which included the secretary in Mr. Bevill's local office, another friend of Mrs. Bevill's, and the editor of the *Cullman Tribune*. The visit had been specially requested by Mrs. Bevill whom I knew through her writings for the *Cullman Times*. She knew me

through my column for the same newspaper and the
two history books I had written on one of the twelve
counties in her husband's district.

I remember that from the beginning the visit was a
delightful and congenial affair. I felt as though I had
known these new friends all my life. Conversation
flowed freely and easily, touching on everything from
life in Washington to writing. Mr. Bevill's secretary
and my mother had been classmates in grammer
school, and they enjoyed reminiscing together.

Then, suddenly, the room was electric with the
dramatic and captivating turn of events in Mrs.
O'Rear's condition. She spoke with simple sincerity
in the most radiant tone of voice I had ever heard.
When she finished, everyone began to bombard her
with questions, so eager were we to know every detail
of her amazing experience. (At our invitation, she
later told her story before a packed house at our
church and also before the newspaper editor's
Sunday school class.)

I felt an exciting change begin to take place within
me that day—a change which I could not explain. It
was as if an undercurrent was pulling me with an
irresistible force toward an adventurous journey
such as I had never known before.

God used this little social get-together to show my
guests and me a firsthand glimpse of his mighty
power. It was like the fragrant breath of a rose Oliver
Wendell Holmes speaks of in the poem quoted at the
outset of this chapter. I had never questioned the
healing power of God, but here was a demonstration
of that power.

I had ceased asking God to heal me because I had
long since decided—not without much anguish and

bitter tears—that if God wanted me paralyzed and dependent on others for my personal care, then I'd play the game of life, as it were, with chains on. I would put all my faith in his coaching and try to do the best I could with the restrictive rules.

In Proverbs 20:24 we read: "Since the Lord is directing our steps, why try to understand everything that happens along the way?" (TLB). When I first became bedridden, I prayed daily that God would heal me. I envisioned rising up and walking as did the man by the pool of Bethesda. Jesus' question to him, "Wilt thou be made whole?" always brought to mind physical wholeness.

I wanted desperately to be healed, and I believe in miracles. I believe, too, that God uses medical science and dedicated doctors to help bring about healing. I had been dramatically healed for short periods following surgery at NIH. I have, likewise, experienced emotional and spiritual healing through the years. These experiences cannot be explained by mere coincidence.

But now, hearing Mrs. O'Rear share her remarkable healing, even though I had already been depending on God to supply my every need, I came to realize more clearly the even mightier forces waiting to unleash their power in my life through the as yet untapped circuits of my faith.

God, in his mercy, had looked ahead and seen my need for stronger currents of faith, and then he proceeded to install the channel through which I would receive them.

Six months later, the time had come for me to go to the nursing home. It was a Friday morning, and there was a knock on the door.

Who was coming right at this moment, I wondered? The house was already filled with relatives who, because I had pleaded with them not to cry, mostly had gravitated away from my room to other rooms in the house. With tension thick enough to slice with a knife, my family, heeding my wishes, were keeping their emotions in check admirably as they helped complete the last minute preparations for my departure. Someone opened the door, and my pastor stepped inside.

I had called my pastor earlier to discuss my future plans and to request his prayers. I had not known that he was coming to see me off, but this was just the gesture I needed and was typical of his thoughtfulness. Once again, I sensed that special fragrance of friendship, like the breath of a rose.

I sensed immediately that this dear friend had been sent by God in answer to my prayers that I not make the situation any harder for my heartbroken parents and relatives. Later, in reflecting on the conversation Reverend Masters and I had that day, I could not recall his exact words, but from the depths of his own great faith he had impressed upon me the importance of looking at what was happening in a positive way.

"God loves you very much, Margaret. He knows all about your needs and your ambitions. You will find some way to continue your writing, and perhaps you will have even greater opportunities to serve God at the nursing home than you have had here at home," he told me.

While he led in a prayer of thanksgiving and petition for faith and strength that each of us might face whatever lay ahead with hope and courage, I strongly felt God's presence in the room.

Later, I could only marvel at the calmnes which pervaded my whole being as I was being carried to the car. The hysterical parting I had feared did not take place. To be sure, my heart was breaking, but I felt that God was firmly holding the pieces in his hands, and I knew—truly and assuredly—that with him all things are possible. Even the mending of broken hearts.

*And, behold, I am with thee,
and will keep thee in all
places whither thou goest,
and will bring thee again
into this land; for I will
not leave thee, until I have
done that which I have spoken
to thee of. (Gen. 28:15)*

# THE BOOK OF LIFE

When I entered the nursing home on that cold December day in 1975, I had no way of knowing how closely God's words to Jacob would apply to my own life or how unexpectedly they would be fulfilled.

As previous mentioned, 1975 had been an incredible year bringing as it had a full gamut of extraordinary events and along with them the full scale of emotions from exhilaration to crisis. Year's end found me going forth to a "new land" and faced with the challenge of making a new life for myself among strangers in alien surroundings.

Ironically enough, although I did not see the connection with Jacob's experience at the time, my own journey into a strange land began literally with a pillow like stone. When I was first placed on the little bed that was to be my new home, my head touched the hardest pillow I have ever encountered. The pillow thus became my first problem, albeit one of the easiest resolved. After being replaced by my own feather pillow, the "stone" became a monument on the top shelf of my closet.

Some of the other problems I encountered during those first few days of residency were not quite so simply resolved. Almost immediately, I was confronted with a situation involving the preparation of my food that soon developed into a crisis. I almost collapsed from sheer hunger before the problem was fully understood and remedied.

I can feed myself but, because all the food must be sucked through a tiny gap between upper and lower molars on the right side, it must be blended perfectly smooth to the consistancy of mashed potatoes, or ice cream. Even a tiny lump will clog my miniscule eating space. There is no room for variation. Too thin, I cannot hold food on a fork because I must point the tines downward. (A spoon or straw won't work.) Too thick, and the food can't get through.

The problem was further complicated by the fact that it was Christmas week and the chief dietician to whom I had explained the situation had gone on vacation. The kitchen help was obviously trying hard because the food they served me was nicely blended for people who could open their mouths, but not enough for my tiny opening. Sometimes there were one or two items on my plate that I could manage fairly well. Other times, there would be nothing at all so I would just drink milk and juices and hope for better luck at the next meal.

Since I am not a hearty eater anyway, the skimpy meals did not bother me at first, and I was sure they would get better shortly. But when they had not improved much by the end of a week, I began to get noticeably weaker. One morning I awoke to find that my hand actually trembled when I tried to hold a glass. My family brought food from home several times the next week, but I discouraged this practice in the interest of working things out with the kitchen. Gradually, the situation did improve and, while there would always be many things I could not eat, I no longer got hungry.

Other less critical frustrations popped up to tempt me to despair. On New Year's Day it seemed that everything that could go wrong did. In the afternoon, when my visitors had left, I suddenly felt defeated and exhausted by lack of proper nourishment. Unseen by anyone, I wept bitter tears. But in the midst of my utter dejection, I suddenly heard a voice say quietly, "Margaret, why are you crying? You are not alone. Trust me and I will help you."

I knew this was the Holy Spirit speaking to me, and I was instantly ashamed as I realized my lack of faith. "Lord, forgive me," I prayed humbly. "I don't want to become a chronic complainer, and I know you have a better solution. Please show me what to do and give me strength and patience to cope with or accept these little problems that hinder my comfort or annoy me."

That was the first and last time I allowed myself the destructive indulgence of self-pity while I was in that nursing home. I was glad that the nurses, who from the very beginning had been kind and eager to learn to do things the way I had been accustomed, had not witnessed my little outburst. As the evening shift passed my door one by one and gaily called, "Happy New Year, Margaret," my spirits lifted. I knew that with God's help I could make the new year a good one. I silently resolved to do my best.

New Year's Day is a gate between the past and the future. When one discards the old calendar with its 365 pages of permanent records that can never have so much as the dot of an "i" erased and replaces it with a volume of equal thickness containing the blank pages of, as yet, uncharted days, it is only natural to indulge in a review of the past and attempt a bit of stargazing into the future.

As I lay alone in new surroundings, I thought about the "Book of Life" series which each of us is writing. It may not be bound in leather or contain exactly what we would like, but one thing is sure—its 365 pages are not blank. Outstanding or mediocre, happy or sad, dull or exciting, it cannot be revised. Good or bad, progressive or regressive, fruitful or wasteful, enriching or detrimental, each year's deeds are recorded for posterity. The Bible tells us that God is also keeping a written record also which is called "the Lamb's book of life" (Rev. 21:27). I prayed that the plot of my life would be permeated with an ever-increasing faith in God and that I would write the chapters in my life with a definite goal in mind and illustrate them with courage, determination, and optimism.

In his book, *The Ballad of the Running Man,* Shelley Smith observed: "Life is like a game of chess in which there are an infinite number of complex moves possible. The choice is open but each move contains within itself all future moves. One is free to choose but what follows is the result of one's choice. From the consequences of one's actions there is never any escape."

I fell asleep that first night in the new year of 1976 with the assurance that God himself was going to direct my moves. Isaiah 26:3 says, "Thou wilt keep him in perfect peace, whose mind is stayed on thee: because he trusteth in thee." That kind of peace is a safe pillow on which to rest one's head.

*Now no chastening for the present*
*seemeth to be joyous, but*
*grievous: nevertheless afterward*
*it yieldeth the peaceable fruit*
*of righteousness unto them which*
*are exercised thereby. (Heb. 12:11)*

# RIGID BUT NOT UNYIELDING

At first I worried about how I could tactfully suggest certain procedures to the nurses without seeming too demanding or hard to please. They, too, were unsure of how to proceed and were afraid of hurting me. I was touched by their concern, but at the same time, I was amused and relieved. Here was something I could deal with readily because I knew I wouldn't break that easily. I came to realize that most of these compassionate people had had little experience in caring for someone as rigid as I, and I thanked God for the growing relationship that inspired one of these new friends to confess her fear, thus bringing the problem to light.

The nurses knew little about my disease and the nature of it other than that it was very strange and rare. Out of politeness, they had refrained from bombarding me with personal questions to satisfy their curiosity. I had also refrained from volunteering any information because I had long ago resolved not to bore people with a recital of my case history accompanied by its peculiar pains and problems (unless they showed a special interest by asking specific questions). Now I realized these attendants really would like to know, and needed to know, and so, along with instructions as to the best way to turn and dress me and position my back and hips properly, I began to tell them something about the disease and its effects.

The nurses were as startled to learn that I had perfect feeling in all parts of my body as I was to discover they had thought all along that I was numb. "I have feeling from my head to my toes. I can't scratch myself, and I can't comb my hair. I can't brush my teeth. My jaws became rigid in 1960. My taste buds are normal. I've not had dental care in years, there is no way." I thank God I've had no pain or problems with my teeth—surely this is a miracle in itself.

I explained that my muscles have all turned to bone, which accounts for the rigidity. "Daddy says I'm tireless, I simply don't get tired. I'm not on any medication."

At the time I entered the nursing home I had been having severe pains in my right leg for more than a year. The slightest jolt or movement caused fiery darts to race through my hip and knee. This was the attack that finally put an end to my sitting in a chair because forcing the hip into a sitting position was unbearable. It was impossible to turn me without some pain, so I tried to grit my teeth and ignore it as much as I possibly could.

Every day in the nursing home brought new friends and new experiences so there was little time to dwell on my problems or to feel lonely. I usually spent the quiet evening hours after supper reading my Bible and reflecting on the day's events. I resumed my old habit of waking up in the morning wondering what surprises the day might have in store.

I was touched by the thoughtfulness of many of the residents who frequently dropped by for brief visits. One of my next-door neighbors was a lovely 93-year-old lady who came every morning to smile and say hello. Although I couldn't speak loud enough to carry on a conversation with her because she was very hard of hearing, we were able to communicate. Another sweet little lady, who had been there nine years and who spent her days performing small tasks for the other patients, sometimes brought her crocheting and sat with me for awhile. A Catholic, she always helped push wheelchairs to the Protestant services and then came to sit by me during the Sunday services since I couldn't leave my bed.

Another resident often brought visitors to my room. At first I thought they were his friends, but later I learned that they were mostly people whom he met in the solarium where he spent much of his time. He always told them, "You ought to go and meet that young woman in room 327. She has written two books about Cullman County." Because of this man I met several new people every week. Many of these people were pastors who had come to visit a church member. Some were history buffs who had read my books. Some seemed a bit embarrassed at what they feared might be an intrusion. But I didn't mind these interruptions. They often led to stimulating conversations which delighted my still-active reporter's instinct that had led me to many interesting stories during my years as a newspaper columnist.

One night I saw two little boys about eight and ten years old pushing my Catholic friend through my open doorway. I had not seen them before, and there were no other adults in sight. The older boy remarked that they had come to the nursing home to sing for a mid-week service. I was sure their parents would be wondering where they were. "We will go get Mamma and Daddy and come sing for you," one of them volunteered.

They dashed up the hall; however, since it was already nearly church time I didn't expect them back. But in a few minutes they were back with their handsome young parents in tow. The father introduced himself and his wife, giving only their last name. Then he asked if I was the author of the local history.

I learned that he had just returned from a trip to the Holy Land. He volunteered to show me his slides on their next visit. After a few minutes, he hesitantly said that his young sons had come and told him they wanted to sing for my friend and me. It was church time, but he stood the boys on a chair at the foot of my bed and, we were treated to a brief concert of contemporary gospel songs by this talented and charming family.

"Did you hear the concert we had in here?" I asked some nurses when they stopped by a few minutes later.

"No. We were coming back from supper and saw Dr. Dunn and his family leaving your room. Did they sing for you?"

I had no idea this kindly young man was a doctor. I was doubly moved by the thought of such a busy man's taking time out at the end of his long day to come to the nursing home with his family and bring cheer into our lives. The thoughtfulness of this family is a perfect example of how God sends unexpected events into our lives to bring renewed hope and inspiration in surprising and heartwarming ways.

*Samuel then took a stone and placed it
between Mizpah and Jeshanah and named
it Ebenezer (meaning, "the Stone of
Help"), for he said, "The Lord has surely
helped us!" (I Sam. 7:12 TLB)*

# A STONE OF HELP

On the first morning after my arrival at the
nursing home, I was suddenly startled to hear a
man's voice outside my door loudly repeating the
Lord's name in vain over and over using one single
profanity. I caught a glimpse of a wheelchair and
recognized it as belonging to Harvey (not his real
name), my neighbor across the hall. I listened as a
nurse called him by name and tried patiently to find
out the source of his frustration. Every question was
answered with the same profanity.

Later, several staff members came individually to
apologize and anxiously urge me not to become upset
by these outbursts. I learned that Harvey had been
shell-shocked and had sustained severe head injuries
in World War II. He now wore a steel plate in his
head. He could understand everything that was said
to him, but he never uttered a word except "Hey"
when he needed assistance. He never bothered with
his signal light. He vented all his emotions from
anger and irritation to excitement and pleasure in
one profane utterance. Sometimes, he would sit in his

room and repeat it loudly over and over for no apparent reason.

Everybody seemed to ignore Harvey's outbursts, and he apparently took little notice of anybody else. Several times a day he would leave his room and go and sit quietly at the nursing station a short distance up the hall. I soon became fascinated watching him painstakingly maneuver his wheelchair into a position to close the door to his room each time he left. He never forgot, and woe to the cleaning lady or orderly who entered in his absence and forgot to shut it again. He also insisted that it be left open an exact number of inches when he was put to bed promptly at seven each night.

Harvey had never given any sign of acknowledging my presence, so I was startled one day to catch a glimpse of him in my little mirror sitting in his room pretending to hold a mirror at the exact angle I was holding mine. He had apparently determined all by himself what I used it for, and now as he became aware that I had seen him, he grinned bashfully and waved his hand ever so slightly. I waved back at him, laid my mirror aside, and went back to my writing.

A short time later, Harvey wheeled himself across the hall and hesitantly entered my door, pausing to wait for an invitation to come. Somewhat astonished, I greeted him warmly and welcomed him in. As he pushed his wheelchair alongside my bed, I noticed a box of chocolate-covered cherries in his lap.

"Oh, no," I thought desperately. "If he offers me that candy, how will I ever make him understand that I can't eat it!"

Sure enough, he set the box on the bed beside me and indicated that I should take some. I couldn't reach the candy, and I didn't want to hurt his feelings. As I wondered what to do, Harvey grasped the problem and set the box up on my stomach, smiling broadly at his perceptiveness.

"Thank you very much, Harvey. I'm sure I'll enjoy this, but I'll have to wait until the nurse can help me because I can't get my hand to my mouth," I explained.

I laid the piece of candy on the over-bed table I kept pulled within reach at all times. Harvey indicated that I should take another, and when I protested that was enough, he insisted. I took another piece and thanked him profusely. About that time, a nurse passed my door, and I saw her quickly backtrack and do a double take. Harvey's back was to the door, and he was unaware of the nurse's standing there, mouth agape. I discreetly signaled that everything was okay.

After that, Harvey began coming across to my room three or four times daily, always bringing me fruit or candy or nuts. I accepted his gifts politely because it seemed to give him a great deal of pleasure. He never found out I couldn't eat them.

At first, my conversations with Harvey were mostly monologues. I would comment on the weather or compliment him on his new haircut or ask a simple question. He listened attentively, laughed aloud when he was amused or pleased, and increasingly uttered short replies to my comments. By listening very carefully I could understand most of what he said, but sometimes I had to guess. He grinned devilishly if I missed his meaning and turned my efforts to understand into a teasing game which delighted him immensely.

I also chided him about his profanity. "Harvey," I
would scold after he had engaged in one of his tirades
just before coming over to my room, "I heard you out
there just now. Didn't I tell you not to say that. Say
'holy cow' instead."

The idea amused him, and only once, after I had
asked him if he had enjoyed his lunch, did he swear in
my room. Apparently, the fish at lunch had dis-
pleased him very much.

Harvey was fascinated by my mirror which was
probably what had attracted him in the first place.
He understood my need for it and frequently took it
out of my reach just to tease me. To his great delight, I
went along with the game and pleaded with him to
return it, which he always did before leaving.

One day, he pointed to my Bible and said, "Holy
Bible."

"Yes, that is the Bible. Do you want me to read to
you?" I asked. He shook his head no, but his words
were a happy sign of progress.

Harvey always left if anyone else entered my room
but the staff expressed amazement at his neighborli-
ness toward me. "It's the first time we have ever seen
him respond to anybody," they said.

In the beginning, my friend, the owner of the
nursing home, expressed concern that Harvey's
frequent visits might be bothering me. Sometimes
they did become a bit taxing and interfered with my
writing when he stayed for long lengths of time, but I
didn't have the heart to discourage this tiny spark of
sociability, however feeble it might be.

Shortly after I left the rest home my family doctor,
who was also Harvey's doctor and who once found
him in my room when he came to check his patient,

teased, "I hear you found yourself a boyfriend."

"Oh, yes," I grinned. "Harvey brought me goodies three or four times a day."

"You know," he said seriously, "you were really good for that poor man. I had never found him in such a relaxed and happy state of mind in all the time I've been treating him."

I remembered then what my pastor had told me about being able to help others, and I knew that my time in the nursing home had been well spent. What might have been a deplorable situation was miraculously turned into a blessing, and my feeble act of charity had been more than amply rewarded.

I had been at the rest home about six weeks when my father found a lady to come in twice daily to care for me. Three of my aunts, who had been especially upset when I moved away from home, volunteered to take turns helping to put me to bed at night. At first, I was reluctant to accept this arrangement because I knew mother would never again be able to assume any responsibility for my care. I did not want to impose on my relatives, but out of their love for me they insisted that it was the right thing to do.

"But you can't go home now. We are just beginning to learn how to care for you right," some of the staff protested when they learned of my plans to return home. Certainly, these people who had become dear friends in a few short weeks and with whom I had developed a warm relationship, which in turn had enriched my life in many ways, would always remain an indelible part of my life. In many ways, it had been a profound experience—one that I would never have chosen voluntarily, but also one that I can truly be thankful for.

The serene faces of the elderly residents as they sat in Sunday morning worship services; the gentle old man who walked up beside my bed in the back of the chapel and whispered quietly, "God bless you"; the little old lady who softly took my hand and said, "Honey, I'm so sorry you can't walk"; the inspiring bi-weekly hymnal singings and the dedicated lovers of gospel music who came from miles around to bring joy to the residents; the heart-warming and totally unexpected reception I received one night after a friend in the singing group dedicated a song to me and the people who recognized me as the author of the county histories came one by one to greet me; and Kara, the little 11-year-old girl who devoted two evenings a week to doing small chores for the residents—these were some of the things that worked together for good according to God's purpose (Rom. 8:28).

Out of my weakness came amazing new strength surging from the depths of untapped inner resources which opened doors to fresh insights into God's ways. Out of my fears came a greater maturity of faith and trust. Deeper than I had ever known and clearer than I had ever seen, the substance of things hoped for had become things evidenced, and it was almost as if I now walked by sight rather than by faith.

# OUT OF WEAKNESS STRENGTH

On the day I came back home, I received a letter
from the publishing company to which I had
submitted my first novel for consideration. They
were enthusiastic about the humorous story based on
facts in the lives of my paternal grandparents and
their fifteen children who grew up on a farm in North
Alabama. The editor was asking if I could
add another hundred pages, so I immediately set to
work.

In the meantime, mother's health began to decline
steadily. By December 1976, she was in critical
condition and underwent exploratory lung surgery
which disclosed a rare type of lung inflammation. Two days later, she suffered a mild heart
attack.

She was given massive doses of prednisone for the
lung ailment which in turn caused excruciatingly
painful muscle spasms in her back. Already in great
pain from rheumatoid arthritis, she now became
almost helpless and was bedfast much of the time
during the summer and fall of 1977. She fell into a

state of depression induced by the drugs she was taking for her lungs and became badly discouraged.

Under these circumstances, the pain and distress became more than she could bear, and she often lay in bed and wept bitter tears of frustration. Neither I nor my precious father, who is a great optimist, could say or do much to lift the spirits of this one who had for years encouraged me so strongly.

It was, I knew, going to be a lonely battle in which she would have to map out her own strategy and fight her own battles with God's help. I longed desperately to add the soothing balm of massage and hot packs to my words of encouragement. I was unable to do this, but I had foreseen her need for something she could do to keep her thoughts from dwelling too heavily on her infirmities. Her favorite hobby had always been gardening which she could no longer pursue. Now, I reached far back into my memory for the technique of crocheting, which I had not been able to do for more than fifteen years. I instructed her verbally in every tiny detail of each stitch and watched very closely through my mirror to catch and correct any error until she had mastered the basic stitches. It proved to be good exercise for her fingers, and she whiled away many hours making afghans and cushions for friends and relatives until cataracts, another side effect of the prednisone, forced her to stop early in 1978.

The brochure which the druggist had tucked into one of mother's bottles of prednisone had warned of a long list of serious possible side effects. It soon became obvious that she was developing some of them, but her doctor told her it was the only medication available for her lung inflammation. The dosage was heavy, but the specialist cautioned that she might suffer even more dire consequences if she discontinued it abruptly or reduced it faster than his prescribed regulation.

As the muscle spasms produced pain of growing intensity, she became too weak to sit up or get out of bed without help. Over and over she questioned whether the aid to her lungs was worth the constant pain in her back. Finally a boned corset did enable her to get up without help, although she was still in pain and unable to do much.

As the weeks stretched into months, Daddy's optimism never faltered. Each morning as he dressed Mother, he encouraged her to have more hope and look on the bright side. Even under the tremendous pressures of caring for Mother, preparing breakfasts and suppers (and lunch on the four days each week he isn't at the stockyards), tending his cattle and other farm chores, along with various household chores, gardening, and lawn upkeep, he was a pillar of strength. Somehow, he found a bit of humor in the midst of tight schedules and weariness. Our friends were always marveling at his fortitude and lack of complaints.

One day, an attractive friend of mine from high school days visited me and found Daddy trying to mash my dinner fine enough to eat.

"You know," she smiled, "the reason I never did marry again was because I couldn't find a man like your daddy. I never have heard him complain about anything."

Daddy laughed, a bit embarrassed. I told her the nurses had already suggested he get a job as an orderly.

My father has always expressed his faith more by

actions and general attitude than by words. Many are the times he has said to me, "If only you didn't have to be this way," or "If you could have walked, you and I would have done such and such." As much as possible, he made me a part of the farm life he loves so dearly, discussing problems and plans, joyously announcing the birth of a new calf, appointing me secretary to keep account of his herd of registered black angus cattle, whose pedigrees require enormous documentation.

Daddy is also a realist and a man of great reason. He accepted our situation as something that had to be lived with as best we could and was content to leave the outcome with God. His philosophy is that life is simply too short to be wasted crying over things that can't be helped and worrying about things over which we have no control. The miraculous strength that enabled us to see the vital need and importance of remaining strong for mother's sake, as well as our own, and the ability to laugh at the blunders which Daddy and I made in our novice roles as cook and household manager could only have come as the fulfillment of God's promise of strength for every need.

There is an inspiring story of an old sea captain whose ship became fogbound far out at sea. A devout Christian, he did not pray that the fog would be suddenly lifted because he knew enough about weather conditions to know that this would be contrary to the natural laws of nature. Instead, he prayed only that no matter how long the storm lasted, he would weather it, and no matter how long the fog held, his ship would make it through.

This simple prayer of faith and trust has deep

meaning for all of us who at some time in our lives find ourselves fogbound by troubles and trials, temptations, guilt, sorrow, and despair. Often we can only see darkness but we need to remember that "The light shines in the darkness and the darkness has never put it out" (John 1:5 TEV). We must keep in mind that while God sometimes calms the storm, he also sees fit sometimes to let the billows rage and only later to bring calm to the storm-wracked passengers.

We must understand that although we are battered on every hand, the hold is taking in water faster than we can bail it out, our strength has ebbed, and we are in danger of sinking, we are still in God's keeping. He will navigate the course and bring us into the right port.

It is never easy to pray "Thy will be done." We may be guided into a different harbor from where we had set our sights, but the experience is far richer, challenging mind, body, and soul to their greatest potential.

I was keenly disappointed when the book publisher which had praised my novel so highly returned the revised version containing the additional one hundred pages they had requested with the objection that it "was too much of a good thing." I had received many rejections, but never one quite like that. I wasn't sure just what the editor meant, but I promptly got busy on another revision and fired it off to a new publisher.

It has been apparent for quite some time that the surgery for the removal of the fibroid tumor, which had been postponed in 1975, was becoming inevitable. The tumor was enlarging, and the pain was often savage. To avoid becoming nauseated and risk the possibility of getting strangled, I was sometimes forced to skip a meal altogether.

Dr. Frank Stitt, Jr., who is one of the most highly skilled surgeons in the South, and who had accepted my case after the death of his father, could not be sure how much, if any, of the problem was due to an invasion of myositis ossificans progressiva into one or more of my internal organs. I was aware that, due to my paralysis and complete immobility, the surgical risks were higher than average. I did not dread the surgery nearly so much as I was concerned about possible post-operative complications, especially of strangulation if I became nauseated by the anesthesia.

The greatest fear, however—and the one that caused me to hesitate the longest—was that something might go wrong which could lead to permanent bladder and kidney problems. I had always had perfect control which enabled me to follow a schedule requiring only part-time nursing care at specific times three times daily. The inability to follow such a schedule on a regular basis would most likely mean a catheter or a return to the nursing home, neither of which I wanted if they could be avoided.

My constant prayer was that, when the time came, I would have the strength and courage to face in a truly Christian way whatever happened, good or bad—even death if that was part of God's plan. I wasn't afraid of death because I knew I was ready to go, but I did not want to die just yet because there were still too many things I wanted to do.

Finally, two weeks before Christmas 1977, pain

won the battle. Silently uttering a prayer surrendering the last of my fears to Christ, I called Dr. Stitt and he promptly admitted me to the hospital.

After a battery of tests and X-rays, I was scheduled for surgery on Monday before Christmas. On Saturday, Abbot Hilary Dreaper and Brother Joseph of the St. Bernard monastery, both cherished friends, came bearing a beautiful poinsettia plant.

"Margaret, we will have some of the monks in the chapel all day on Monday praying for you," Abbot Hilary told me after giving me his blessing.

Sunday afternoon brought a steady stream of visitors, along with word that several churches in the communities surrounding Baileyton had requested special prayers for me. About mid-afternoon, during a brief lull of visitors, the phone rang. It was a long-distance call from a minister whom I had first met some months earlier when he and some of his congregation had traveled from another city to pray for my healing. Now, he was asking if he could have prayer with me over the phone.

Mixed in with the visitors were nurses with pills (which had to be pulverized and dissolved in water) and papers to sign and operating room technicians with questions. But even in all the chaos and excitement, I began experiencing an unexplainable sensation and became aware of an unseen Presence hovering near me. I could not then adequately describe it and still cannot except to say that it was very real. I had a strong desire to share what was happening with anxious relatives and friends, but, at the same time, I knew it was still too fragile, too personal, to put into words.

While I was having supper, two friends from a town

more than forty miles away walked through the door saying that my pastor had called them. The extraordinary day, already abundantly blessed, was fast jamming the circuits of my memory with events, the significance of which would become more precious in the days and weeks ahead.

But there was still more to come. Later in the evening, the brother of a friend and his wife came to wish me well. I had never met them but I felt that I knew them anyway. More than a year earlier, Mr. Craft had become a victim of the Gullian-Barre syndrome that had swept the nation in the wake of the swine flu vaccination program (although he himself had not received an innoculation). For many weeks, he had lain at the point of death and the disease had left him totally paralyzed.

A devout Christian, he had never given up hope. He was now confined to a wheelcair but, after long weeks of patient therapy, he was slowly regaining the use of his arms and hands. I had once written him a note of encouragement, and now he and his lovely wife had come to assure me of their prayers.

I was deeply touched by their kindness, well aware of the extra effort that had been put forth by both of them on this bitter cold night. Proudly and humbly grateful, Mr. Craft spoke of his long ordeal with no trace of self-pity, showed me the progress in the use of his hands, and talked optimistically of his efforts in learning to walk again.

After they had gone, I meditated upon that miracle and the amazing events of this day in which I had walked in the presence of God. I looked over at the sleeping pill which a nurse had brought earlier and laid on my nightstand. I knew that, even though I

would be required to swallow it, there was no need for
I was at perfect peace.

Then one of the floor nurses, who had cared for me
on a previous night, came to prep me for surgery.

"Margaret, your face is positively glowing. You
must know Jesus," she said.

"Yes, I do, and I'm not afraid," I replied quietly.
I dozed off to sleep thinking of her remarks and how
marvelous it was to be able to answer affirmatively.

The last thing I remembered in the operating room
was my throat being swabbed in preparation for a
tracheotomy after two anesthetists had tried unsuc-
cessfully to insert a tube—which seemed to be as big
as a water hose—into my nose. When I woke up, I was
being wheeled out of a door, and I thought the
surgeon had just finished the operation. A clock on
the wall said 1:30 P.M., and I remember thinking,
"My goodness, I've been in there over six hours. I
wonder what on earth they did to me." Then I lost
consciousness again.

The next time I awoke, I was shivering uncontrol-
lably and vomiting violently. I was aware of several
nurses working frantically over me. My poor daddy,
looking gray and shaken, was standing at the foot of
the bed smiling at me. I tried desperately to tell them
I was freezing, but only an unintelligible jumble
came out. They began to play a guessing game and
finally hit on what I was trying to say.

Daddy took my hand and made me understand that
I was in the Intensive Care Unit (ICU) and that
everything had gone fine during surgery. I slept
again and when next I opened my eyes my brother
Bob thrust my little mirror at me. I declined my
mirror thinking this oddly amusing, but was too

groggy to laugh. The following day, when I mentioned the incident to a nurse, she laughingly told me I had sent him after the mirror. Later, back in a regular room, I was cared for one day by a vivacious brunette who revealed that she had talked to me constantly all the time I was in the recovery room. When I asked her if I had wanted my mirror in there, she assured me I couldn't have cared less what was going on. I never recalled even being in the IUC.

By the morning after surgery, the nurses could translate a few words of what I tried to say. When I managed to greet the doctor intelligibly and tell him I was feeling good, he looked startled.

"My! My! You are sounding real good," he exclaimed.

"Good? I sound horrid. Nobody can understand half of what I say," I croaked. (It was impossible to read my paralyzed lips.)

"Oh, yes, we can. You are doing wonderfully well. Most people can't utter a sound with that tube in their throat, but we don't tell them because then they won't try," he explained.

Of course I hadn't known that, but it did explain the amazed looks I had noted on the faces of the nurses when the shifts changed. And it did put a different perspective on the situation. I recalled that Daddy had always insisted that nothing could shut me up. While I didn't sound too good, it was sure great to be able to speak at all since I couldn't shake my head yes or no.

When the anesthetist dropped by, he grinned at my attempt to talk and pronounced it fantastic. I chided him for giving me such a hard time in the operating room.

"You know about that?" he asked in surprise. Then he went on to explain that they kept getting the tube into the wrong passage because my neck was so rigid and were finally forced to do a tracheotomy.

In addition to a hysterectomy, Dr. Stitt had done a biopsy on the rectus muscle and examined my internal organs for evidence of myositis ossificans. On Wednesday morning, he came into ICU smiling broadly.

"Good news, Margaret. The tumor was massive, but the tests now come back negative and so has the biopsy. Your internal organs are all in fine shape, and there is no evidence of myositis ossificans."

It was the best Christmas present I could have received. Once the tubes were removed from my throat, I had no difficulty breathing. I was uncomfortable but at no time did the pain ever approach pre-surgery intensity. I only required one injection for pain after leaving the ICU forty-eight hours following surgery.

No efforts had been spared by either of my doctors or the hospital staff to prepare for any complications or for my personal care and comfort as I recuperated. My recovery proceeded wholly uneventfully. My relatives and friends, doctors and nurses, made no attempt to conceal their amazement.

"Margaret, you are far ahead of many of our hysterectomy patients so soon after surgery. You are making wonderful progress," the nursing supervisor remarked one night.

The unexplainable sense of expectancy, of feeling that an unusual experience was happening to me, that had first begun on Sunday grew even stronger after surgery. Lying quietly in ICU, I had the opportunity to explore more deeply the events of the last few days and the impact they were having on my life. The scores of prayers that had been raised on my behalf were being dramatically answered before our very eyes far more exceedingly abundant than we had dared ask or think.

I had asked for strength and courage to cope with the inevitable discomforts and pain. By Christmas morning, six days after surgery, I knew beyond any doubt that I had received far more and that a truly miraculous healing had taken place. It became perfectly clear that the many things which now fitted together as a chain of events could only have been providential.

None of the things I had feared most had materialized. I felt great! I also began to understand perhaps why God doesn't often see fit to bestow miracles instantaneously and dramatically. The indescribable impact on the mind and emotions are too overwhelming and exhausting to grasp. Instead, God waits until that time when we are willing and able to do his will and use what he grants for his glory.

It was literally impossible not to share this experience with my visitors and with those to whom I wrote notes of appreciation for the beautiful flowers, cards, and many other kindnesses shown my family and me. I sensed that an unseen force outside myself was irresistably compelling me to do so.

It was following this surgery, after I left the hospital, that Dr. Morris, who assisted Dr. Stitt with the surgery, obtained information on research that had been done on myositis ossificans (see chapter 6).

More and more I was glimpsing firsthand God's

mighty power moving on my behalf. I thought back to June 1975 when Mrs. O'Rear had come into our home and my life. That day something within me was deeply stirred, and the circuits of my faith were infused with a mighty charge. I was seeing the effects of that in my life, and my gratitude knew no bounds.

*Keep your feet on a steady path, so that the limping foot does not collapse but recovers strength. (Heb. 12:13 Phillips)*

## CHOOSE LIFE

Not long ago, Washington syndicated social columnist Betty Beale reported what she described as one of the strangest anniversary celebrations ever held in our nation's capital. It was held for one hundred and fifty guests who had been invited by Administrator of Veteran Affairs Max Cleland to celebrate the eighth anniversary of the loss of both his legs and his right arm during the Vietnam War. The injuries that almost cost him his life had been sustained when Captain Cleland bent down to pick up a grenade which exploded in his hands.

The idea for the party was Mr. Cleland's own. When someone asked him why he wanted to celebrate a horrible tragedy that left him confined to a wheelchair for life, he explained simply, "That's the day my life was saved. Somehow, you come out of it [tragedy] with an appreciation for life that is incomprehensible to the average citizen. You learn the things that are important. Life is precious—and friendships."

And so instead of wasting his life in bitterness, he

grabbed this new challenge by the reins and set forth with determination. After years of surgery and recuperation spent in hospitals, he was elected to the Georgia State Senate. He later ran for lieutenant governor and was defeated.

At the 1978 Annual National Prayer Breakfast attended by President and Mrs. Carter and more than 2,500 members of Congress, the Cabinet, and ambassadors from around the world, Mr. Cleland, the guest of honor, spoke humbly of this defeat.

"A young man on the way up, I was suddenly on the way down. About that time I came to the end of my rope and I had to confront myself, my fellowman and my God. I had taken control of my life and run it into the ground. I prayed, 'God forgive me,' and then let Him take me. Then I had peace in my heart," Mr. Cleland told the hushed audience.

Shortly after this defeat for lieutenant governor, he was asked by President-elect Jimmy Carter to head the giant Veterans Administration Office. A man who might well have been lured into the deadly clutches of self-pity and become just another statistic was instead celebrating a nightmarish event that in a matter of seconds had not only changed the course of his life, but had given him a whole new roadmap. In choosing the boulder-strewn mountain path of perseverance over the valley road to despair, he recovered strength of body, mind, and soul.

In the book of Ecclesiastes we find these words: "God's ways are as mysterious as the pathway of the wind, and as the manner in which a human spirit is infused into the little body of a baby while it is yet in its mother's womb. Keep on sowing your seed, for you

never know which will grow—perhaps it all will"
(11:5-6 TLB).

Max Cleland kept on growing the seeds of courage
and initiative, and they led to a presidential
appointment. Not everybody, of course, reaches that
prestigious plateau, but we never know which of our
many experiences are going to be the most fruitful.
Careful examination, however, will show that things
which once seemed meaningless or unbearable have
a mysterious way of preparing and strengthening us
for richer experiences.

The pain we have endured enables us to better
understand the suffering of others. The heartaches
and tragedies we confront inspire us to take a closer
look and apply deeper thought to the priorities we
have established. The frustrations that confound our
dreams and ambitions help to undergird the beams of
new bridges so that they will span the deep waters
that cross our paths. The insights we gain, the gifts
we discover and put to use, the courage we cultivate,
the defeat we resist—all contribute to the successful
germination and nurture of the seeds we sow.

The masthead on the *Alabama Wheelchair Society
Magazine* carries the quotation "When God closes a
door He always opens a window." As editor of this
little magazine from 1968 through 1974, numerous
stories of remarkable courage springing from the
eroded fields of misfortune and hardship came to my
attention to prove the truth of this saying. People
who had been knocked down by the storms of life,
swept away by raging waters, as it were, and cast into
the midst of thorny problems, fought their way out of
physical poverty and emotional ravages to a life of

fulfillment, leaving enrichment in the footsteps of their strengthened feet.

Broken pieces were picked up, dusted off, and creatively reassembled or recycled. The problems and circumstances of these people varied widely and often seemed hopeless; the methods that enabled them to overcome and achieve were frequently unorthodox, invariably daring, and sometimes—like Dr. Hartman's sightless trek through medical school—trailblazing.

But all these people who defied the raging storms and rooted out the thorns shared at least one important thing in common. They had a deep-centered belief that life has more purpose than merely serving as a wasteland for pain or a warehouse for worry and despair. Pain may be a constant companion. Despair may be a powerful temptation. But the tiny flicker of mystery that staunchly illuminates a reverence for life which transcends the ravages of tragedy exerts a greater pull.

Henry Ward Beecher has written that "God does not ask us whether we will accept life. That is not the choice. The choice is how."

In the Old Testament book of Deuteronomy is found the story of Moses exhorting the Israelites to obedience and laying before them the conditions for restoration and blessing. He concludes his exhortations with a challenge that has reverberated across the centuries: "I call heaven and earth to record this day against you, that I have set before you life and death, blessing and cursing: therefore choose life, that both thou and thy seed may live" (30:19).

The choice is always ours. God is not going to force

himself or his will upon us. We can soar on the wings of God's promises, or we can sink into the quicksand of hopelessness. We can tackle mountains with faith and trust, or we can languish in caverns of darkness. We can walk through the valleys on crutches of boldness, or we can flounder in the quagmire of bitterness. We can be consumed by despair, or we can be open to opportunity.

The Old Testament prophet Isaiah assures us there is unflagging assistance and strength for accepting the greater challenge. "[God] he will be very gracious unto thee at the voice of thy cry; when he shall hear it, he will answer thee. And though the Lord give you the bread of adversity, and the water of affliction, yet shall not thy teachers be removed into a corner any more, but thine eyes shall see thy teachers: And thine ears shall hear a word behind thee, saying, This is the way, walk ye in it, when ye turn to the right hand, and when ye turn to the left" (Isa. 30:19-21).

Because this blessed assurance has been indelibly written on the signposts of every detour along life's pathway, our limping feet can recover their strength on the new soil of our transplanted lives.

Many times we are faced with situations and circumstances we can't do anything about but which God expects us to exercise our faith and do something with. But we cannot get on the right path until we have accepted the detours that have forced us off the superhighway, leading straight to the ambitions and goals of our dreams, and onto the bumpy sideroads that take us first through wildernesses of trials and troubles, sorrows and frustrations.

Acceptance of these stumbling blocks doesn't mean that we abandon the journey and claim squatter's rights at the roadblock. To accept adversity is not to be weakwilled or powerless or resigned to a barren existence. Rather, acceptance is the possession of an expectant hope, an undercurrent of indefinable anticipation, a receptiveness that frees one from the bonds of fear and conquers pain and disappointment.

It is not enough that we be content to say "Okay, Lord, I'll accept the burden of this imposition you have sent me," and then condemn ourselves to a life of impotence and meaninglessness. Genuine acceptance is going a step further and putting the hardship to its most effective use.

It is not enough that we simply make the best of our adversity-restricted resources in an attitude of passive surrender. God intends that we should be content only with *making* the most of them. Paul's imprisonment did not signal his retirement from spreading the gospel. At times he was on the pinnacle of joy, at other times in the valley of despair. But he always persevered. I am always encouraged as I look at the life of this apostle. God gave Paul the victory over all things—even the possibility of death itself—in spite of the fact that he was often very weak and human like us.

Many of Paul's writing were written under great stress, but he always confronted the issues squarely, and we see the power of the cross and the energy of the Holy Spirit at work in him. Four of Paul's writings are called "The Prison Epistles." He seized his imprisonment as an opportunity to witness to his guards. Denied access to audiences, he persevered under difficult—but no less fruitful—conditions. His letters breathe of confidence and strong personal commitment. The dominant note of these letters is joy. Likewise, the abundant fruits of fulfillment that yield an ever-deepening faith and stronger trust spring from our willingness to be put to the test and nourish the roots of our adversity however rocky the soil in which they have been transplanted.

A shrub that has been transplanted from the fertile soil of a nursery to a location with shallow sandy soil suffers a great shock to its root system. Whether it lives and thrives, or dies, depends upon the remedial action and attention given it by the gardener. Left unattended, it will become stunted and unattractive, unfruitful, and robbed of its potential. Fertilized, mulched, pruned, and watered, it enriches its surroundings with its beauty and fruitfulness.

Plunged into the arid soil of tribulation, choked by weeds of self-pity, infested with depression, the human spirit soon becomes blighted and robbed of its potential. Rooted in faith, nourished by the promises of Christ, cultivated with trust, we, too, can take hold and send our pruned branches stretching forth in new and better directions. Just as the deep roots of a twisted and gnarled old tree enable it to withstand the howling storms of Mother Nature, so can our own strong roots bear up against the hailstorms of doubt and misfortune.

The apostle Paul tells us how to insure strong roots—be rooted and grounded in Christ's love (Eph. 3:17). The qualification for a strong witness is that we be "rooted and built up in him, and stablished in the faith" (Col. 2:7). Paul's meaning is that our roots need to go down deep into the soil of God's marvelous love (TLB).

Sometimes the "Why?" of tragedy gets in the way of "How?"—how to be an overcomer, how to be a joy-bearer, how to radiate our convictions that God hasn't made some awful blunder in our lives. If we are not careful, we become so preoccupied with what we feel is the unfairness of it all, dwelling on the bleak outlook, that grasping the means of rising above the thing that has deterred or altered our course is neglected.

The questioning of the why of tragedy or illness or sorrow which has seemingly ruined our lives is only natural. It is the obsession with searching for a reason or bitterly denouncing and blaming God for our afflictions that halts our growth and our hope and quest for a fulfilling life.

Usually growth is gradual. It came to me that way. Gradually, through reading the Bible, I began to see that God does not plan for us to be healed of all afflictions. Not that he wants his children to suffer, but that he wants them—and those around them—to know that his grace is sufficient for *every* need. When Paul wrote that God's grace is sufficient, he wasn't just mouthing nice-sounding words. I have already referred to II Corinthians 12 where the Apostle exhorts us to glory in our infirmities so that the power of Christ may rest upon us (v.9). "Therefore I take pleasure in infirmities, in reproaches, in necessities, in persecutions, in distresses for Christ's sake: for when I am weak, then am I strong" (v. 10). Here is our answer to the why.

I know now that wholeness is not so much in having perfect health as it is in being in harmony with God and obedience to his will. Whenever I read or hear that passage in John's gospel—where Jesus asks the man at the pool "Wilt thou be made whole?" (John 5:6)—my thoughts now flood with the many ways in which we can experience wholeness.

The Bible reminds us repeatedly of God's unsearchable ways in such beautiful words: "O the depth of the riches both of the wisdom and knowledge of God! how unsearchable are his judgments, and his ways past finding out! For who hath known the mind of the Lord? or who hath seen his counsellor?" (Rom. 11: 33-34).

The Bible gives us many interesting examples of God's unsearchable ways. You may recall that when Pharaoh let the Israelites go out of Egypt, God did not lead them by way of the land of the Philistines which would have been the easier route (Exod. 13:17-22). Nor did God choose to let Paul remain in Tarsus for ten long years preparing for the tasks that lay ahead of him before having Paul embark on his missionary journeys.

All through the Word of God there are promises of strength to run the course and stand firm in the storms, but nowhere does God promise an obstacle-free course or a cloudless way. Proverbs 16:9 reminds us that "A man's heart deviseth his way: but the Lord directeth his steps."

In one of her books, Corrie Ten Boom writes that "God has no problems, only plans." Faith in God does not offer a guarantee that we will be healed of all afflictions or protected from all sorrow and tribulation. It does enable us to make sense out of adversities and triumphantly conquer them.

No matter whether our approach is made on the firm steps of well-being or the limping feet of affliction—or maybe an inability to use one's feet at all—just around the corner, just over the next hill are unspeakable riches, surprising and fulfilling, for those who cling to their faith in a God who knows what he's doing.

William Arthur Ward, a noted author of inspirational articles, has written that faith can transform doubts into discourses; obstacles into opportunities; conflicts into challenge; grief into gratitude; sorrows into springboards, and limitations into launching pads.

Not only is Jesus Christ our Lord a stone of help, he is the mortar that bonds the broken pieces of shattered, lonely, sinful, and desperate lives into beautiful mosaics of peace and joy. He is all in all, totally adequate.

| | | | |
|---|---|---|---|
| MAR 23 '80 | | | |
| | | | |
| | | | |
| | | | |
| | | | |
| | | | |
| | | | |
| | | | |
| | | | |
| | | | |
| | | | |
| | | | |
| | | | |
| | | | |

92
JO
Jones, Margaret Jean

The world in my mirror

1241